The Inn

(The First Book)

By: Sadegh Sarouy

Translated by: Pitter Saloon

Edited by: Majid Jafari Aghdam

Title: **The Inn**

Author: **Sadegh Sarouy**

Translator: *Pitter Saloon*

Edited by: *Majid Jafari Aghdam*

Cover: **Mehdi Alvandi**

Publisher: **Supreme Century-USA**

ISBN: **978-1939123848**

Acknowledgment:

My debt of gratitude goes to Mr. Soheil Pirbastami, the head of Yassi Foundation in Iran, for his support and kindness.

The book dedicated to Heidar, my late uncle.

O' young man, this body is like an inn

Every day, a new feast is visitant in

Hey, do not say it will be a burden for me

Since it will instantly fly into nothingness

Anything comes along from the occult universe

It is a feast for your heart, welcome it.

Jalāl ad-Dīn Muhammad Rūmī

Part I

It All Began by the Breaking of the Jar

The inn is located on the edge of a sand sea. It stands strong like a lighthouse. If someone looks at the east from the inside, he will see the Obliso. On the other side of Obliso, another mountain has soared high, the Third Mountain.

Behind the Third Mountain, the plain extends to far aloofness, up to the point where the gray silhouette of the town seeps into the mirage.

The lands on the north of the inn are covered up with a forest of the salt tree, tamarisk, and Alhagi[1], Maurorum bushes.

On the south, a narrow and long road twists and turns like a snake between the nameless sand dunes and branches into three other pathways right before the inn;

An asphalt paved road to the harbor,

A dirt road to Zakaria,

And a faded out pathway to nowhere!

---

[1] . Alhagi is a genus of Old World plants in the family Fabaceae. They are commonly called camelthorns or manna trees. There are three to five species.

At the locus of this arid geography, in the recess of a sad plain, under the roof of an old inn, facing the empty window stands a lonely boy.

In order to know more about his situation and to understand what is concealed in his eyes, we have to travel to the past. The journey to the past lands is like gathering up spilled water and returning it to the broken jar. It is not impossible but very difficult!

However, we will do it. We will restore the precious broken jar to its original state with our magic and we will pour the spilled water inside it to the very last drop.

Well, let's cut it short and cautiously go back to the shattered jar and the spilled water.

*****

The last missing piece

The sun rises in a large gap in the middle of the mountain. It shines on the clothed wall. It crawls down its length and shows up on the window pane, this is the beginning of the day and it is accompanied by a promise for me.

It stepped into the room like a transparent ghost. It cast itself over the brown wall, passed by the metal folding chair, walked slowly on the rug, then went around the room and sat on the plastic stool next to the bed. It whispered in my ear, "You had promised to tell me about it."

I need to restore it to its first day conditions right now.

Something that has missed its path, its memory does not recall the subject matter and now, every piece of it has been thrown to a corner.

I need to collect tiny crystal pieces from all corners of the room.

Some of them have fallen on the carpet, several pieces behind the chair, under the stool and at the corner of the room. . . and other hidden places.

I find something on every corner and I feel happy.

Of course, one is always concerned about what if the last piece could not be found?

*****

The Silk Road

Traveling with me – perhaps – could be a bit boring and troublesome. I am afflicted with arthritis disease. To the extent that sometimes it is difficult for me to walk. The occasional headaches have driven me and the people around me up to the wall. But . . . with all these misfortunes, I am a frequent traveler.

Alright! We are going to travel to a specific place at a specific time. We are going to find the thing that was left behind - maybe due to distraction and hurry – on the metal chair of the railway station waiting for hall. From the loudspeakers, the last warning about boarding the train trots around the hall like an invisible horse. It goes through the hall and finally vanishes into the train hull:

"Dear passengers! The train is leaving the station. Please get on the train instantaneously!"

A noisy hubbub fills the hall. The last warning is always followed by a hubbub.

The train begins to move like a black, sleek and experienced horse. Its big wheel rotates slowly. The water steam gushes out from both sides of the locomotive and the entire station drowns in a thick fog; the stone steps, metal chairs, huge luggage carriers who are waiting for the next train, luggage and cargo carts, shiny and slender metal beams that at their highest point end with a large cubic lamp whose four rectangular glass sides cast its yellow light to the surroundings on four directions. Graystone platforms and the large clock in the middle of the railway station hanging from its high ceiling.

The light approaches from the opposite side. It brightens up all corners. Sparks fly out in the battle between the iron wheel and the iron rail, they pass through it and instantly diminish.

We pass by the window of the last settlements in the present time and also pass in front of the large title engraved on the metal plate.

There is no lasting scenery on a journey. The sound of change in the nature of epoch makes one's body to shiver.

We reach the magnificent extension of the silk. That great old road. The passageway that in the past times, caravan after caravan of camels was flowing on its bulk. Once, the smell of its spices and the perfume of its aqua rosé made delighted the people. The camels have held up their noses, pushed out their chest, and have gradually disappeared in its historical dust – due to the horror of a dark and daunting plain.

No sound mixes with the other, the time passes, time passes, time passes. . . and oh! I found another piece. On it, an image is painted that looks like a caravanserai. . . or. . . a. . . an inn!

A light is approaching from the opposite side; it brightens up everywhere and suddenly fades ******

The Inn and the Silence

The sun illuminates the gray-blue sky and pours light on the ground. Its sharp and shiny rays force the old man's wrinkled and burned eyelids to close. He blinks repeatedly and his pale gray and sleepy eyes go undercover.

Niyaz, drawn into himself and bent forward, is sitting on a smooth boulder located on the short and old hill. The landscape in front of him consists of a long, narrow road that twists and turns behind nameless hills, and after a monotonous extension along the edge of the sand sea, branches into three pathways in front of his hereditary inn; a road to Zakaria, the other one to the harbor and the third one to nowhere.

The third road, which in fact – just – a faded out path of a forgotten past, extends from the back of the inn to the forest. After a brief passageway through the salt tree and tamarisk shrubs turns toward Obliso and then fade away just before reaching Obliso.

Niyaz and the people of that area believe the third road is cursed.

The dull look searched for something in the distance. Niyaz's deep-set eyes were accustomed to the bright sunlight, to the sand and soil and to being expectant. His eyes are desert's eyes.

The inn is his enclave and refuge. He returned to the inn. He poured tea for himself and drank it while still hot to avoid delay in the daily work. He swept clean the vacant place of his guests, that is, all of the inn's lobby. Then he dusted his royal chair and the small decorated desk that he had inherited from his father. He wiped the glasses and panels with a piece of soft cloth.

After doing all of that, he retreated to his secret hideout.

The chamber at the end of the coffee shop - a secret door - [after that] the narrow and short corridor, and finally the den!

He kindled a fire in the brazier, put the wire over it and shortly afterward, the old innkeeper, wrapped in the opium's gray-white smoke, and was reeling in nothingness. The euphoria's spider web spun around his frail body and his hands sunk into goo.

Outdoors.

The sky was spreading to eternity in an unpleasant brightness. Smooth and flawless. Free of clouds and dust. There is no traveler in the desert area whose arrival could make us feel good, like seeing a dark spot at the remotest parts of the boundless sea that would make one expectant. A traveler who bangs on the coffee shop's door or anything else that breaks this monotony and hush.

However, we have not come here for this, to watch Niyaz and his frailty, or sand dunes and endless territory and the silence of the sand sea . . . We are here to find the last piece. So, we leave Niyaz and the hideout and other things to themselves. From among the three routes, we choose neither the road to the harbor nor to nowhere; but we will choose the one that leads us to the beginning of the story.

Part II

The Secret of the Gypsies

(The Unwanted Gift of Fate)

"Satan himself deceived a woman called Hobart(Lilith). He slept with her and made her pregnant. The Devil named the child that was born from that intercourse, Obel II."

For years, the Gypsies, according to an old tradition, went from one village to another and from one oasis to the other. They could do with a piece of bread, a bucket of yogurt, a bowl of butter and a jar of *dough* (yogurt mixed with water).

Most of them were middle-aged men and middle-aged women. Sometimes, one could spot a young man among them, and more or less an old man or an old woman. The natives said they would never die.

What were the secret of their loose red shirts, long green shawls, and blue and yellow skirts and pants that expelled death?

Up to that particular day, no one had ever seen Gypsies with a newborn baby. But this time, the baby's cry could be heard before they stepped into the village. The red, green, blue and yellow colors encircled the well. They took bucket after bucket of water out of it and filled their flasks. Then the colors turned toward clay and straw plastered houses and some houses to get various items. By the way! Other than the usual things - things that could be eaten to survive - they asked for milk. So, while they were dispensing silk and cotton fabrics and diabolic and rare items among the people (plaster statutes of naked angels with dark and guilty wings, or two lovers under a large umbrella, photographs, and postcards with provocative images of coy half-naked women, etc.), they were asking for a nursing woman. And of course, the true seeker will find.

Bara'at Sufi was one of the elders of that small village. Three months ago, his wife, Khanom, gave birth to a boy, notwithstanding that she was closer to being an aged woman rather than a middle-aged one.

The family's paternal lineage was weird. Bara'at's father, Noroozkhan, suddenly disappeared after his marriage. There was no sign of him for months, and after he resurfaced, he did not make available any explanation. He disappeared again a few months later and returned several months after that. This story continued until he went away in harsh winter and did not return. His father's father was an **ecstatic dervish**, and he was waiting for **salvation** until the end of his life. The situation was the same even prior to Bara'at's father and grandfather. Restless, ecstatic and frenzied people.

Bara'at himself was a cold-blooded and calculating person. In fact, he had nothing in common with his ancestors, and according to his headcount and calculation, this last baby was redundant!

And the fate ruled such that a baby must be weaned from the low-hanging breasts of an old woman, fall into a well, and then cling to another woman's chest.

Very soon, the blue, green, yellow and red colors gathered behind the earthen embankment and went down a new road.

Near the water well, which was located on a short platform, next to the sheep's cement watering trough, the tiny hands of an infant were instinctively and inadvertently waving in the air. An unknown smile was agape between his red and burned face.

He grew up in a land where he had no kin. He grew like a weed and became taller. He took root in a land of not his own. He lived with the people who had no feelings toward him.

Where did the Gypsies go? To somewhere else, to another plain, another village, another well; and followed their ancestors' paths. Those vibrant colors went away from this land. Like butterflies that in the earlier springs blended the colors together between the earth and the heavens and created something new. They had gone from this place, and there was no turning back.

A few years after that, the village people - good or bad, white or black, man or woman, with all sorts of standing and status - disappeared in dust and black magic. Cholera wiped off the life from a couple of villages.

Khanom (Bara'at's wife) reluctantly and apathetically breastfed the Gypsies' gift.

Bara'at and Khanom's last child had a beautiful smile. It was like the blossom of the colorful flowers in the first days of May, at the time when the sounds of goats, lambs, men, and grass were mixed, and the sky reached the peak of its blue hue.

His eyes, at that very young age, encompassed the flash of a hundred galaxies. He opened them, it was daylight; he shut his eyelids, darkness fell.

******

The Demonic Boy, a Remnant of the Caravan of Colors

"Hug me; love me, even as much as your sheep and dogs . . ."

The people thought of him as a Gypsy child. The devil's offspring! Although he had no name, they called him by many names; crazy child, black-forehead child, Gypsy child, Jinn child, demonic child, and . . .

We must come clean that his behavior influenced the choice of these names. But the strongest reason was that the people thought he was a child of the Gypsies, and an expelled child, ominous, unwelcome, and spellbound to an eternal curse for that matter. The arrival of hard and gloomy days also escalated the sense of premonition. Cholera was approaching. The drought lasted long. The plight drove the people up to the wall, and everyone was desperate.

During such days, the brick kilns were constructed in the heart of the desert. The long brick pole of the kilns sprouted out of the earth and the lengthy shadow of each of them, cast a black and ugly line on the ground.

The demonic boy was the first child to be rented to the brickworks!

The kilns' huge smokestacks were a nightmare for the demonic child and the other kids. There were other nightmares too; heavy and large molds, a hot ground where the bricks were left to dry up, and the kiln itself . . .

Other children were rented to the brickworks one after the other. Their parents thought they had to do this. But in the case of the demonic child, they did not need any justification. He did not belong to any of the inhabitants. A kicked-out stray dog, always starving, always alone. He paced back and forth all day and night in the boundless extent of the desert - with a lame leg and defective waist - among the foxes and jackals. Under the hot sun and on the baked sand.

Did the same things make him go berserk? Or did he smash his head to something when . . . who knows?

See the water inside the magic jar, the wavelets that escape slowly towards the sides. Each wave returns joins the other wave and runs off again. In the midst of these interactions, the face and stature of the demonic boy are reflected on the water;

A bare ass, shredded shirt, crying boy. Homeless and hapless. A dog with no owner that messes around . . . that's it!

He was 5 years old when he started working in the brickworks! He was alone, stuck in the triangle of the brick pole nightmare, the ever-hot ground, and the kiln, a dragon whose mouth was always ablaze.

Seven years passed in that manner. Seven years of bootless brick molding.

For seven years, experiencing the most unbearable human pains, hunger, thirst, getting cooked in the heat, waist and leg pains, which would crush down a big and strong man, let alone a fragile and weak child.

Seven years! No rest and recreation, no visitor, no acquaintance.

After the demonic boy, each of the other innocent kids entered that hellhole with eyes that were nearly popping out of their sockets by terror. One of those innocent children was the one we were looking for.

In a dim and dense night that you could not see your own hand a few inches in front of your face, and the darkness was such that it crushed one's chest under high pressure, the demonic boy decided to jump over the wall! He was not alone in that historic night. Another boy accompanied him: his brother. Both had been breastfed by the same breast.

They had grown up together and now they were inmates together. Although the kid was afraid of the demonic boy's blood-ridden eyes, nevertheless he preferred his company.

Facing them, the tall wall. Beyond the wall, barking of the dogs and howling of Jackals.

On this side, slavery, forced labor, and bondage - on the other side, an unknown world and unpleasant feelings that are only known to someone who has jumped over the wall.

*****

The Demonic Boy - A Life Story

Life begins with pain and suffering. Suffering from pregnancy and birth pangs, and if this birth occurs in the year of measles and cholera, the pain is another kind of pain and the suffering, another kind of suffering.

In that year, many newborn babies were buried under the cold ground in large numbers and many men and women dived into the land of the dead. Cholera and measles joined forces to conquer the villages, one at a time.

The child that we call the demonic boy came to the world - or to put it more precisely, was thrown into our world - in such conditions, by an old and poor couple. The aged man and woman were afraid of having another baby. Perhaps they could not stand to witness the suffering and death of another child. The disease monster was peeping behind every door and was alert, with an ear to the wall. Maybe an extra eater in such a situation would eliminate the others' chance of survival. Perhaps they had noticed something in him. A curse... a black spell . . . and what not . . .

The old man and woman decided to suffocate the baby under the pillow, but out of the blue the old woman fainted and the old man blacked out. So, they drew another plan to get rid of that curse;

The crone wrapped the poor child in a four-color shawl. The old man threw it over his shoulder like a bundle and went out. The dessert spread wide before him and in its limitless extent, he faded out of the view, limping bit by bit.

Ancient people in dry and waterless lands excavated many wells in the desert with the hope of finding water. If they hit the water, that place thrived. Petite agricultural lands, simple mud houses, the sheep and the people, encircled the well; and if there was no hope, they abandoned it and tested their luck elsewhere.

The old man was looking for such a dig-and-go well in the desert wilderness.

Sooner rather than later, he found a well in the middle of a short and wide hill. It was the real deal. An abandoned and waterless well.

He quickly limped his way to the well opening. He held the baby with a shaking hand over the well and stayed motionless for a while. What was he thinking about?! Nothing. He heard the child's shriek but did not listen. He saw the child but did not look, as if he had not seen anything. There were no feelings in his deep-set and dull eyes.

The soil was sprayed on his white and long beard and had turned to mud close to his lips. The wind flapped his long and loose shirt and his full beard . . . he let it go! He let go of the baby.

The old man stumbled and was about to fall into the well. Fistfuls of dirt were poured on his face and eyes. As his right hand was in the air, this time, with a gush of wind, he was thrown to the bottom of the hill from the top.

The dust became the wind. Storm. Everything turned to the color of the dark soil and was impressed with revenge. The howling of the wind and the wrath of nature . . . screamed in the old man's ear.

His eyes were filled with dirt. The holes of his nose, mouth, and ears.

He was hidden from the eyes like a memorial that no one remembered anymore, and retreated in the mind of the history, went far and disappeared.

The anger diminished as if nothing had happened. Everything calmed down. A gentle breeze slightly moved the finer sand.

After a while, a shadow fell on the well. Other shadows followed suit, and one by one appeared on the well opening. A group of colorful desert hikers circled around the abandoned well.

Their women were tough. Rough skin, large nose, wide eyebrows, and long forehead, with red and wrinkled faces. Big and tall. The men were black and slender. Their heads were small and their faces were round and tiny.

What beautiful outfits! Every piece of them was a season in a faraway part of the world. Four glossy and neat colors.

These gorgeous people always on the go could never ignore a baby's cry at the bottom of the well.

A man from the group went down the well - a not-so-deep well - and emerged with the help of his relatives while grabbing a blue dirty baby. The child was neither crooked nor there was a sign of ill omen on its face, and also it did not carry a spell or a curse. It shrieked vigorously as if it was under great pain. That newborn was only a baby with curious eyes, wrapped in a colorful shawl.

That multihued shawl was a sign that it might have been of the same tribe and ancestry of the Gypsies.

Part III

The First Meeting in the Quiet Morning of the Coffee House

There is forever and a day a hidden place. Not to store a precious or scarce thing or a safe and sound have to be protected from the natural or human enemy. No! This hidden place is at the remotest spot and is not readily available all the time. That place can be a chamber to chill out. Where one may change his pants without the fear of being exposed!

The Niyaz's hideout was also neither a shelter for security nor a hiding place for a treasure and jewelry. It was only a dungeon. A den for comfort and ecstasy.

These are all that is there in the hidden chamber;

A simple and four-sided brass brazier that Niyaz inherited from the father. A rotten yellow and worn out broom that seemed to be his own age! An old and rough straw mat. A chest in the mysterious closet. A broken and corroded mirror, hanging from the bare mud wall that Niyaz sometimes looked at himself in it. In a hangover, he saw a man with a slanted felt hat, running nose, tearful and colorless eyes, and a loose and dull face. In euphoria, he saw a man with a round felt hat worn properly on his head, shiny and puffy eyes, a red and juicy face and smiling lips.

These were all of Niyaz's personal items. They cheered up the old man when he was tired of standing up and staring at the mirage distortion and the eyes that fought the dust.

It was two hours after sunrise. The old man next to the brazier was struggling with a great deal of grief and depression. He saw himself helpless and desperate, "I will die right here!"

His eyes were asleep, and if he did not feel that a traveler was on the way, he would certainly allow his eyes to fall asleep in that wrong time.

He crawled disconcertedly out of the hideout. With that khaki shirt and gray pants, he looked more and less like the desert. Like the desert soil and sand.

At the back of his mind, he suspected the death of the old lady. Why did not she cry out at night? Where is that old and impatient goat to nag to Niyaz and disrupt his euphoric nap?

These thoughts brought a faint smile to his dry lips and he whispered, "Have you ever seen any old woman die that effortlessly?!"

Niyaz passed through the narrow corridor and reached the secret door. The door that allowed him to enter the coffee shop. It was silent, and seemingly that day would be a very unruffled day. He paced through the corridor created by the layout of the tables and chairs. He glanced with sympathy and respect at the *Uncle Hookah* painting (the painting was a well-known image of an old man with a white beard grabbing a hookah straw and looking ahead with a faint smile.)

Niyaz opened the door and the golden bell that was placed above the door tinkled. He stepped on the wooden platform. He suddenly panicked and began to agonize. His body shuddered and his heart nearly stopped beating.

Two unconscious and soiled kids were crumpled to the floor in front of the door, like two electrocuted pigeons.

The Desert Prophets

What happened to the boys?

Did they escape?

They fled, but where to?

Jumping over the wall is just the beginning of the story, thereafter is blackness and homelessness. Ordeal and unnecessary suffering and fear!

The lad followed the demonic boy. The two walked on and on through endless darkness without rest and without stopping for a moment. The lad was following his stepbrother. The demonic boy sniffed the desert soil like a dog. He changed his path at any point that he felt they should turn away. In the darkness that terror had filled the lad's eyes, brain, mind, and psyche; the demonic boy howled or growled and made scary faces. So, there was a good reason they called him demonic boy! He absolutely went over the top when they reached a typical hill like hundreds of other sand dunes. There was a well in the middle of the hill. The demonic boy sat next to the good rim and began to howl. He went around the well opening, jumped up and down and screamed. It was not clear what would have happened if the storm did not approach.

Perhaps he would fall head-on down the well. The hurricane was going to take the two boys to the air with itself. They were lucky to fall from the hilltop into a not-so-deep pit.

After the storm, the fight began anew. The two passed through the snakes and scorpions. They were thirsty and hungry. Sometimes they fell down and sometimes they were totally hopeless. But throughout the way, an unseen and invisible guide advised them, 'Toward Obliso,' and they unwittingly followed the right path. Gradually, they found themselves on an old road. A faded pathway and a shadow, the remainder of an old road.

The demonic boy constantly repeated, "We will die, we will die of thirst!"

That ancient faded out pathway gradually merged with a real road. The newly-discovered road twisted and turned like a snake between the sand dunes and reached an old building. Just before reaching the building, the boys went belly up in front of the wooden staircase due to extreme fatigue and thirst. If the old man had decided to mind his own business in euphoria and engage with his own self and the world of his fears and thoughts or to fall asleep, the two innocent children would have surely died under the hot sun and on the sizzling sand.

Niyaz quickly took both of the boys inside the coffee shop. First, he placed the demonic boy under *Uncle Hookah*'s painting and then carried the lad in his arms, ran inside the coffee house and placed him at next to the demonic boy.

As his hand touched the boy's back and he felt his heartbeat, a sensation ran down his dry veins. Unconsciously, a smile appeared on his cracked lips. He brought a bucket of water and immediately poured all of the water on the unconscious bodies of the two kids, regardless of wetting his antique carpet. Suddenly, the children jumped up and came to their senses.

"Mahrokh! Mahrokh!" shouted the old man.

After a while, when he did not receive a response, he grumbled, "Has she ever answered, that you are expecting it a second time?!"

****

In the Sanctuary of the Soul

Someone else was there too.

He sensed the sunlight. He stretched out his arm and touched its heat with five spread out fingers. This is the morning sun!

There were two shadows in the distance that followed the mirage's wavy distortion. The two shadows came closer and closer, and little by little, from a spot in mirage, shaped into two real living persons.

The blind man saw them approaching! He grabbed the wooden pole and used it to stand up. His head and face were covered with a lot of loosely hanging hair. He saw the two children as they fought death, who were approaching while teetering and limping (well, his eyesight was different than mine or yours). The two boys were now just a few steps away.

"Who are you? Who are you? Who the hell are you?" asked the frightened and messed up blind man. All of a sudden, he passed out and fell down from the top of the wooden platform. At the same time, both of the kids also fell unconscious to the ground.

There was a secret in the fainting of that man. A great mystery!

******

Who is Parishan?

"We call him Parishan. The first time we met, he told me he had no name. I asked, 'How on earth, gentleman?' He said, 'Call me Hooy!' When did I meet him? What year was it? It was very hot, god knows. The year Morad died. The year dust rained down on our head from the air and the ground for thirty days.

You be my guest and do not quarrel
The discussion will turn in your favor

I was going mad; all of us were in the same boat. I wanted to kill myself. I wanted to kill everyone around me, and finally myself . . . Our sheep died out. Everything was dark and gloomy. Our situation was bleak. Our life was worse than death. We were unfortunate, too unfortunate. He arrived and addressed me as I sat on a platform, "Do not you want guests?" The crazy wind had disturbed his hair; it nearly tears off his long and loose garment.

I replied harshly and impatiently, "No! Guests are no good."

To be honest, I had shut down that lovely inn. My father's corpse turned in his grave. May God have mercy on all the deceased people; he was very zealous about this inn.

He pulled out a red rose from under the shawl that he had thrown over his shoulder and put it in my palm. I had never seen a rose like that in my life . . . God knows that I saw it only once again thirty or forty years ago, among a foreigner's belongings who our guest was overnight. I had not seen a red color. My hand felt hot by touching that flower. My heart was filled with hope. Fresh blood ran through my veins. Presumably, it was Siavosh, Siavosh . . . I was set ablaze in his presence. I sat down to cry, my wife came and cried at my side too. Then, we heard his voice which was like a sweetly singing bird, "Do you want a guest?"

He looked at the desert wilderness and suddenly the wind stopped, the storm and the twister stopped. The dust suspended in the air settled on the ground. The bad year was over. Just at a glance!

The next time he came to meet me, I realized he was blind, he had no eyes."

******

Faraz, the Hero of Defeat

On the road from Zacharia to the inn, a square-shouldered and handsome man was riding a donkey with only one ear.

A faded out byway imperceptible to a naïve person's eyes like me. He sometimes napped and sometimes whipped the donkey's butt with a pomegranate twig. With a cigar between his lips, exhausted under the intense sunlight, he yawned but was still cheerful. He left Zacharia's village two hours before sunset. The sun was halfway beneath the plain's horizon, as the silhouette of a building's top floor gleamed through the halo of opaque dust across the hills. As he negotiated the curve around the hill, the familiar building, solid and firm, emerged out of darkness: the inn. He cried joyfully and whipped the donkey's butt, and the thrill of arrival made him half drunk and half mad. Meeting the brother, seeing a bright friend, and watching the moonlike face of the brother's stepson.

He is Faraz, Niyaz's older brother. In principle, he should have been heir to the throne and would have inherited the inn. He was the first son and the daddy's scapegoat! But he was adventurous and pigheaded. He was a soaring eagle that did not fit into the cage. A pleasant song that could not be swept under the rug. A love that could not keep calm in the chest.

He was young when he went looking for his fate. He disappeared for thirty years. No news and no signs. In the thirteenth year when he returned, his father had died recently. The mother was spared the agony of the disease in the early years, and Niyaz was the only one left behind. Therefore, he purchased a house close to his brother's, married and kept some sheep. He had five children, four sons, and a daughter. Three of his sons died within a week and one disappeared without any trace.

Among Zacharia's inhabitants, the wolves killed the most sheep in his flock. He always incurred the highest damage by the loss of sheep via disease and plight, etc. However, those few sheep were enough to keep the simple life of the lonely old man running. Yes . . . his wife died too - ten years after children died - and only one daughter remained for him. Faraz believed that the pure girl was totally wasted, "My moonlike daughter, my pretty one, my gem, my ruby, got married to a pile of shit."
He is still immersed in the sludge of losses and regrets, like a naïve Bushlambo[2].

*****

The Null Zone

Zacharia's dirt road was reflected in the dusty window pane facing the sunset. The crimson light shone on ancient and old things that seemed to have been dipped in the sand. Everything was still, except for the reflected image of a rider in the window.

The lad of our story was awestruck in the recess of the sad plain under the ceiling of the inn. As if time did not pass for him. Shortly after the sun descended in the dust, the crescent of the moon appeared. It moved up little by little and a magnificent and shiny star kept pace with it up to the middle of the sky.

Where have we seen this unique and familiar framed image?

Where have we seen this body stuck between death and life, this myth that stands strong?

---

[2] , a type of fish.

We have reached The Null Zone. Our common heart and our memories that are connected together with a delicate and invisible cord brought us here.

Everything starts with naught. From naught, we germinate out of the soil and continue the story. The sun that will arrive the day morrow from afar - from behind the high mountain, from the plane cavity and distant lands - and rises, that sun will not be the one prior to us. Its soothing flame crawls in from every hole and cracks, from the half-open windows, from the open hatches. And how beautiful it is . . . like the spirit of all of our past ancestors.

What the boy is doing? Why is he staring at the distance so silent and still? What is going on outside?

Parishan was standing next to the wooden pole. In a hysterical circulation and rotation.

His right-hand point to the sky, his left-hand aims at the ground, and has surrendered his body to the spin. He is chanting: Ho ... ho ...

A bit farther, a huge old man has arrived on a donkey and makes *ho ho* and *hey hey* sounds like an intoxicated camel and shouts, "Niyaz, where the hell is you, junkie!"

Niyaz gets out of the coffee house and rushes to the brother.

******

The Forename of the Sun
(The First Battle, Dreams, and Nightmares)

The storm is coming. The boy was so immersed in an overwhelming and tumultuous thought that he neither noticed Faraz's noisy arrival nor figured out the sudden disappearance of the sun. In the desert, in the stubborn wilderness, the sun does not leave the sky so easily. A desert dweller knows this well. Many a day, Niyaz sat on his boulder and just the half-burnt sun at the dusk seemed to take its time like the hardest and most difficult of days.

When the last ray of the sun on the wall died calmly, the lad had still stuck his feet to the ground and did not blink. His newly shaved head using electrical razor felt heavy and could not rest on his body.

(Niyaz had a Solingen shaving razor. Every now and then, he seated the little boy on the wooden platform beneath the canopy and shaved his head bald. He adjusted the boy's head with his hand, then the *clunk clunk* sound, 'It is like shearing wool of ewe and lambs, a bit easier, less troublesome, more enjoyable.' Then the morning breeze caressed the back of boy's neck as if a little fairy blew on it and kissed it. A pleasant stinging sensation spun around his head. The wind blew away the cut hair.

However, the poor demonic boy had long hair, long like women's hair. But not *that* soft and delicate, not *that* nice and perfumed, as a matter of course. He had a dirty and disheveled hair. Smelly and with a bad haircut. It reminded one of a monster's hair.

Nightmares and dreams were intertwined in the lad's head. Some of them were bright and hearty, and some black and crooked.

Two people in the vastness of the world can see his thoughts and fancies. One is Parishan and the other - luckily - is me!

I will now give you a brief overview of what is going on in the lad's head. The jar shakes gently. The magical water inside it rippled. A pulse, escape and merge. Circle in the circle. The collapse of the tide and in its center, an image is cast that looks like a jail. A prison with tall brick walls and even taller brick smokestacks that can be spotted from afar. Like a long spike hammered into the straw silo's floor. That place is the brickworks factory. In its vast area, many topless children are busy molding the bricks. Their bodies are fried and sweat is running down their chest, waist, and head. They move large brick molds with plenty of effort and difficulty. A predatory human-animal creature is also running to and fro looking for a child who works reluctantly, sits for a moment and talks to others. He feeds on the children's suffering. He rejoices with the grief of innocent children and his ugly and dirty lips open to a peal of omnibus laughter.

Each brick smokestack is over a big, scary mouth. A mouth is full of flames and fire. It is the kiln itself. The same hell that God has described in his diary.

There are seven kilns in this big brick prison. Seven melting pot mouths, seven blazing hells.

Every and all day this tragedy goes on.

At night, twenty tired and heat struck children are piled up in tight and suffocated quarters. The place is sweltering; the ground is feverish. The smell of sweat and slime choke the kids.

I see the children, each sitting at the corner of his fears. Withdrawn into himself with things popping up in his head. They see a pale image of their home in the dream. Father, mother, brothers, sisters, the sheep, the roads to their villages, hills, and grasses, mountains and valleys . . . and any other pleasant thing. The images and dreams are spinning, rotating, whirling, and suddenly all of the imagery changes. Those hearty images and colorful dreams merge with the living nightmare around them and become a black monster. It shouts and the chains on his hands and feet tinkle, "Fresh human child meat!"

"In difficult circumstances, in bleak days and daunting hours, in homelessness or war, one immerses himself in the simple and anecdotal dreams of the past more than ever, seek refuge in them, asks for help. The dream eventually pales out in the light of the bitter and painful reality of the surroundings and finally, it turns into another nightmare.'

From the dungeon of the lad's thoughts and nightmares, we move to the beautiful plain of his mind:

Parishan, like lightweight and gentle lost butterflies, quietly slipped down from the inn's top floor like turning a page of Shahnameh. Parishan easily found his way though he is blind! As he is standing there with long white clothes and a groomed beard has covered half of his face, he says, "Only the real seers can fly."

The boy felt glad. He was going to cry out of joy but Parishan disappeared abruptly. The demonic boy's face took its place. He laughed and showed his yellow teeth. His face exploded and was scattered in the air like woodchips.

Such is the revolving heavens' manners
You're never sure whether it is unkind or kind
Beware, do not brag about a high throne

Niyaz slapped his palms together and told stories as a stand-up storyteller. He turned around. The Shahnameh tapestry enlivened behind him.

Sohrab is passing away on his father's knees. At another corner, Rostam cuts off the dragon's head. Elsewhere, he rotated his big scepter around his head and bragged:

My mother named me Your Death

The destiny made me your sledgehammer

His two-pronged long, blue beard flapped in the wind. Rostam stopped moving and turning and bragging. He took a few steps forward and pointed to somewhere. The lad followed Rostam's gesture and threw his two shiny brown eyes to that direction like a lasso.

The lad came face-to-face with a dark and creepy building. That building of horrors that was surrounded by a high and awful wall - that unsophisticated structure - seemed to be built on the ruins of an old castle. Neither the beginning of the wall nor the end of it was in sight.

The lad was gripped by a moist and sickening fear. He wished he could escape, but his two legs were stuck in the pitch. All of his limbs were paralyzed. He could not move. The black building shook heavily. As if it was rooted out of the ground. Dust scattered in the air and pieces of rock were jolted to every corner. The walls, its fiery cobblestone pavement, the fences that were entirely cursed spears, moved toward him with all of their bulk. The lad was all alone among them. There was no one to save him. A voice echoed in the area. Someone called him, "Hedayat . . . Hedayat! Hedayat!"

The lad's eyes opened and he returned to reality. It was dark outside the window. It was night. Niyaz was calling him, "Guess who Hedayat is here. It is the uncle, uncle Faraz!"

******

Parishan's Most Precious Asset

The demonic boy used the same piece of wood that he had killed the scorpion with, to turn around the dead carcass of the miserable beast. He shoved the piece of wood in its stomach and pulled it out. He felt great joy doing that.

As Faraz passed around the hill in the twilight after dusk and was on his way to the inn, the demonic boy saw him from the top of the hill. Then, like an arrow leaving the bow, he fled to the inn with that lame leg and defective waist. He did not look back for a moment until he got to the inn. He was very afraid of Faraz. He perceived Faraz as a bad-tempered old man, who was cruel and a bully. As the old man jumped down the donkey and noisily rushed to his brother, the demonic boy remembered to breathe. So, he breathed a sigh of relief. He leaned to the inn's rear wall and seemed to have sunk into the ground. A short while after being relived from danger and fear, in the gentle darkness of the eve of night, he saw the scorpion's glittering back, which quickly ran toward the shrubs behind the inn.

After killing the poor animal and playing with its corpse, he decided to spend the rest of his time peeping at the blind man. That task gave him great pleasure too.

He lay in ambush for Parishan. He used to wait until Parishan fell asleep. He calmly approached him to steal Parishan's most precious thing! The book. He did not know what the book was and what it was for. He only knew that it was more beloved than life for Parishan.

When he was at the closest distance from the book, abruptly the man's eyebrows crawled up and the thin lines on his face changed. It was the moment that Parishan's skinny and bony hand within a very fast reaction, descended on the face, head, and body of the demonic boy with immense power, and he fled from that place with painful groans. But in another day and at another hour, that incident would happen again.

In humans, there is an instinct called Deadly Obstinacy! To put it simply, it is when someone does something and gets punished in return. The punished person does it again and is punished again (and more severely). This is repeated so many times until the Punisher gets tired and loses the game. Just like the unequal battle between the leopard and the unseen mouse! Regimes fall like that. Children get what they demand as such, and many other things. The demonic boy too, got near Parishan's holy book unwittingly and unknowing at least once a day, and of course, was beaten as a result.

And now, for tenths of times, the demonic boy set off for Parishan's resting place to steal the book. He tip-toed such that no one might hear his footsteps. He squeezed his snout on the inn's brick wall and proceeded. In the past, when the wall ended, he reached the wooden pole that Parishan always leaned on it. But this time, his plot was aborted! Hedayat was sitting next to Parishan. The blind man had put his hand on his shoulder with smiling lips. He was cheerful and happy (as if two great lords were giving away hundreds of sheep to each other as a gift) and the lad was also happy and laughed.

There was something much more important and salient going on than the sitting of these two beside each other! The book! The book that had not been seen elsewhere and in the hands of another person save for Parishan was now in Hedayat's bosom!

Faraz's booming and rigid voice collapsed the world over the head of the demonic boy, "How are you, my bright comrade?!"

He sat on his knees in front of Parishan and placed both hands on his shoulders.

The unlucky and starless old man liked Parishan a lot.

The demonic boy was no longer there, he had escaped.

*****

The Holy Book, That Unique Diamond

Let me talk about that holy book:

I do not know at what date was it compiled and written. It is covered with a special kind of leather. It is brown, light brown, and there are traces of Iranian blue color on its edges. The book title is erased and there is nothing left of it except for a golden powder. When Niyaz saw Hedayat's holy book for the first time, he thought that the book was Shahnameh and his heart sunk instantly. He always believed that there was only one real Shahnameh in the world, and his father has inherited it from his ancestors and afterwards, he received it from his father.

However, after a while, he realized that the book was not Shahnameh! And he should not dig it too much. A question popped up in Niyaz's mind. Something that he always thought about it. If that book is not Shahnameh, then what is it? Why that book was so worthy of attention and care? What text other than Shahnameh deserved keeping and safeguarding?

If the rain surprised Parishan on the road, he would hide the book under his worn out shirt. If he stumbled and was falling, he would embrace the book like a baby lest it would be damaged.

To cut a long story short, Parishan treated that ancient old book, whatever it was as if it was more valuable than his life!

And now that precious holy book was in Hedayat's bosom. It was like the most important news in the world, a flash flood that destroyed everything. The Earth stood still, or the sun forgot that its duty is illuminating Earth and other planets . . . !

Calm and cool and indifferent to his surroundings, Faraz was filling hashish in the cigarette that he had already emptied out its tobacco.

From behind two empty holes, Parishan's unobtrusive gaze was fixed on the book like a person staring at a unique diamond. Hedayat could feel the warmth of his unseen gaze on the book. A subtle mental relationship was established between the two.

The disheveled and liberated blind man began to talk, and said, "Read."

******

Transformations

After Hedayat came into Niyaz's life, all of his life changed. The old innkeeper, with joy and smiles and a calmness that was rarely seen before and with great patience, instructed Hedayat how to run a coffee house and what hospitality meant.

Hedayat was one of the three people who were allowed to go into Niyaz's hideout. He read Shahnameh to him and, while reading the Shahnameh correctly, showed the words and vowels to the lad. He pointed at a verse in Shahnameh and asked him to read it;

You proceed with what is expected from the rulers
The father was king and the son is a king too

Prior to Hedayat, the poor Niyaz always thought in his loneliness about the day that his eyes will be dim and his hands shake and his memory destroyed. Who will read Shahnameh to him on that day?... And, apart from that, who will see the stains on the cups and clean them?

And god tossed that nice and cute boy in the middle of his inn.

Mahrokh, who already looked like a dead woman, revived! From a feeble aged person thrown at a corner, from an ever-nagging and groaning old woman, she had grown into a teenager in an aged body and did not fit in that wrinkled and loose fitting garment.

What would she make for Hedayat's breakfast in the morning? What story should she read to Hedayat at night? Oh . . . alas, in the images taking shape on the magical water, I see the separation . . . I see great grief. I see the two who are waiting in sorrow.

*****

Parishan's Session for the Book Reading Ritual

The skinny and wrinkled hand grabbed the gray brick at the corner of the wall. The hand skin seemed slightly darker in the gentle darkness. It was full of brown spots. Swelled veins, like decayed hoses, showed through the loose and drooping skin. They were like long narrow sand streaks in the desert. That hand was Mahrokh's hand. Niyaz's wife and Hedayat's stepmother.

She could not see well in the evening's darkness with her dim amber eyes: shadows that had gathered under the Parishan's light.

The silhouette that leaned on the wooden pole and chanted was that of Parishan. The shadow that had stood in front of Parishan with a book in his bosom was Hedayat. The other two shadows were Faraz and Niyaz, which had just joined the crowd. Two brothers who seemed to be made of separate waists and abdomens!

Faraz was sitting on his knee. He stuck the cigarette butt to his lips and drew three deep puffs. He held his breath. He turned red. His eyes popped out and finally, exhaled the smoke in his lungs with a dry cough.

Niyaz was surrounded by questions, and his eyes were shifting between Hedayat, Parishan and the book, 'Why the book was in the child's hand? Parishan has gone crazy. What on earth does he want from Hedayat? What is written in that book?... Why?. ."

Parishan, quieter than ever, articulated his speech cold-bloodedly (he had shaped his hands as if he was holding a heavy pipe!)

"Dear child! This book is the story of the people who are all dead. That is, their most fortunate one is now lying in the cemetery forever! There are no signs of the unlucky ones. However, they were tortured before they die, and suffered in prison. Chains and locks have punched holes in them . . . or even worse. Of course, a couple of them reached their destination before death . . . where to....!"

It was unclear whether the Parishan's statement ended with an interrogative or declarative tense. He asked as dry coughs had brought tears to his eyes, "Is it a story? A history book? What are these ridiculous things that you saying, maniac?!"

Parishan did not pay attention to Faraz's words.

Hedayat did not know what to do at all. Open the book or not? Parishan had not said anything about that.

Niyaz's throat had dried out because of the desert and he felt all of his body was like a rotten and wasted piece of wood, and now it would shatter in the breeze. He had forgotten to breathe. 'Well, what my lad has to do with these terrible things which this crazy man says?' He wanted to grab Hedayat's hand and escape from there.

- "Read!"

Parishan's prompt brought them all back to reality (except for Faraz who had been stuck in deep delirium!) Hedayat was so taken aback that the book was about to fall from his hand. Where should he read? Parishan moved slightly. He bent toward Hedayat and said triumphantly, "Dear child, as you open the book, you will see a blank page with fine print at the bottom, read that."

Hedayat's hand was shaking. A magical breeze blew from the book to his face. He slowly turned the thick book cover. As Parishan had said, a phrase was written with red black ink in an old and unfamiliar script on the first page of the book. The words were black with a red hue on the edge. It was as if the passage of time had drained the blood from the words. The text was short and very fine, but it was legible: "O' brave man, down with the house of oppression."

The phrase was read clearly and loudly with Hedayat's voice.

Faraz imagined a house built on black wood. Suddenly a hand picked it up, turned it upside down and shook it. Everything that was in the crooked house was suspended in the air! The idea was hilarious and made him laugh out loud.

Parishan was in ecstasy. As if he could not control his hands and other extremities.

Our Mr. Bushlambo stared at Parishan's imaginary pipe. He thought that the fire in the pipe will fall out by the shaking. He wanted to say it aloud. He was going to stop the falling of the pipe fire but he burst into laughter again and could not help it.

Niyaz's world was shattered. Anger, disappointment, fear . . . the nightmares had resurfaced and walked in front of his eyes. They will devour all of his belongings like fire. The inn, the coffee shop, Mahrokh, the hideout, his magnificent Shahnameh tapestry, the Shahnameh itself . . . Hedayat!

The old woman did not know what was going on in that gathering and the conversation. She saw mysterious and dark silhouettes sitting in a circle. The wind delivered the conversation in an undecipherable and vague manner.

One of the shadows separated from others. It came toward Mahrokh. As it got closer, the old woman recognized it. It was Niyaz.

'He has given his book to the kid. What book? A book that messes with your mind.' He struck a match and lit up his cigar, "The madman himself says that everyone who has read it has been tortured, pinned up to four nails, imprisoned . . . killed . . . goddamn Satan... .'

He turned to Mahrokh, "What do you want here, woman?" Many words sprang up in Mahrokh's head; prison, Satan, torture, four-nails pinning, the killed ones . . ."

"Dinner . . ." she said, and then her tongue was locked and she could no longer talk.

Niyaz mumbled in anger, "I . . . I would better eat death . . . watch the guy's blunder . . . he handed the book to a kid . . . prison, torture . . . getting killed or worse!"

He departed from the old woman and went away while still groaning and talking to himself.

The old woman leaned against the wall and slowly sat down. She whispered incomprehensible words, she repeated something.

*****

The Unknown

Last night, after the book reading ceremony - and its adventures - some people entered the inn. Niyaz, who could always sniff the new arrivals, sat on his inherited chair, euphoric and cheerful, away from the recent pique. He only sat on that chair when a traveler arrived or was on his way. The guests were four people, two men, and two women. All four had their heads and faces covered as they arrived. Their dirty and disorderly clothes showed that they were trapped in the desert storm. They removed their covers as they faced Niyaz.

A man with curly short hair and a narrow mustache that had darkened the skin above his lip said after a short whistle showed his surprise, "I could not imagine there is such a beautiful place in the middle of this wilderness."

At first, Niyaz said hello with great respect and courtesy and then said, "As long as I am alive this place will be here, and if I am not, my clever and savvy boy will be here . . . ," then he looked around and yelled, "Hedayat . . . Hedayat!"

Niyaz shifted his eyes toward the afro-hairstyle man and added with an apologizing smile, "However, he is a little playful . . . !"

Were they deserting hikers? Those who go to great lengths to see how a desert night would look? The ones that none may figure out their intentions? Why should one bother so much? To enjoy? From what? From suffering and getting roasted in one of the hottest parts of the world? Whatsoever!

Anyways, they had come and now, they have settled here in Niyaz's inn.

When the holy book-reading ritual ended, Hedayat helped them to take their luggage to their room upstairs.

In the morning, as the sun rose from the edge of the mountain, it first shone on a sixteen-year-old boy grabbing a plastic gun. The plastic gun was a gift from one of the guests of the inn. One of those two women. The boy with a gun in hand had fixed his gaze on the infinity of the sand sea.

He felt strange because Parishan - with his fanciful characteristics - had given him the book to read. He thought to himself about the meaning of that phrase, 'O' brave man, down with the house of oppression!'

The excitement of touching some unknown thing crawled up from the sole of his feet and passed through his thighs and belly. He stroked his chest. It jumped up to his throat and was going to burp out of his mouth!

What was that fresh and frightening sensation?

At that moment, Hedayat found himself in the middle of a strange plot or plan.

The sound of starting the car's engine brought the lad to himself. He saw their jeep departing from a not-too-far distance. He shifted his eyes to the infinity again. The demonic boy appeared. Hedayat could not stand him. He could not stand daddy Niyaz, the uncle . . . he had not eaten nanny Mahrokh's breakfast either . . . just one thing . . .

*****

The Wind Blows In Through the Broken Glass

The upstairs floor is the most important section of the old and small inn. By going up the stairs, you enter a corridor not too tight, not too wide. You will see two wooden doors on the right and two wooden doors on the left. Ground glass was installed on the upper part of all four doors which diffuses the light inside the rooms at night and casts it vaguely on the ceiling. An outdated kitchen is at the end of the corridor. The corridor ends with a broken and dusty window. If you stretch your legs and put an eye at the corner of the window with great effort, you can see the shadow of three people standing, facing the woods in the darkness of the night.

In the morning, the sunlight creeps in from the same partially collapsed window and slowly climbs the wall. At the same time, chatter is heard. The door to a room opens; the man and the woman come out and pound on the door of the other room.

They are the same desert trekkers that have just been welcomed in the inn. They have gathered in room number three and talk about the continuation of their desert trekking.

****

He Approaches the Inn

"Hedayat was in the coffee shop, the people around him were laughing loudly. There was so much smoke in the air that he could hardly see anything. He went around in that ruckus. He turned and turned and turned around and suddenly his hand touched something! The sound of breaking stopped the other sounds. The smoke dissipated and then Hedayat realized what had happened. The glass jar broke! The elegant and delicate jar, part of the inn's legacy. One of daddy Niaz's lovers . . .

Grief pressed on his heart. Water began to flow on the small carpet. There was so much water that the boy thought the inn would drown soon. That intense grief grabbed him and raised him up with itself. Now, Hedayat was the inn itself. From the window (which was now his eyes), he saw the monster that jumped out of blackness with a whip in its hands. The lightning was his whip. Sharp and bright. The monster raised the whip and brought it down on the inn's body (which was the lad). There were storm and fear, loneliness and the pain of lashes . . ."

The lad suddenly woke up. It was dark.

His body was numb! As if it was paralyzed by fear. Two candles were lit up on his face. Gradually, his body loosened up and he could slither on the floor like a snake. Then he managed to walk on all fours like dogs and pass between Mahrokh and Niaz. As he reached the door, he was already walking on two legs like humans. He sank his hand into the dark to find the door handle. After a little effort, he blindly opened the door and a weird shudder shook his body. First, he had to check the coffee shop. He looked up at the upstairs floor. The light of one of the rooms was on.

A few steps away, Parishan's light were on as usual (Parishan's light was actually a lamp hanging from the wooden pole that poured light on Parishan's head. That lamp was always on). Parishan was not there! He opened the coffee shop's wooden door. The little bell above the door tinkled. He felt around the wall and switched on the lamp.

The objects were surprised by the turning on the lamp. He passed in front of *Uncle Hookah*'s painting, through the rows of termite-infested chairs and cracked tables. He walked on the old rug and entered the chamber at the end of the coffee shop. The chamber of samovar and cups. The precious jar - with its illegible blue inscriptions - was at its special and noble place.

The lad calmed down by seeing the magical jar. He returned and stood at the doorframe. He looked at the chairs and the *Uncle Hookah*'s painting that was hardly visible from that angle.

Hedayat was absorbed in imaginary depictions of the previous day: workers whose nose and ears were smeared black were sitting at their tables in silence and fatigue. He counted them: one, two, three, four. Four men, who had sounded the golden bell of the coffee shop at dusk.

Niaz, who could sniff the customers and guests before their arrival, had turned on the samovar. He also had wiped the cups to keep them shining and advised his stepson to clean the coffee shop's floor well, wipe the glasses, and change the burned out light bulb.

Those workers, who our Mr. Hedayat was envisioning, showed up yesterday. They smoked hookah and drank tea. They spent an hour together in silence and went away afterward. No words were exchanged between them. No words other than something like this: it has a nice color . . . it is warm . . . it is freshly drawn.

Hedayat pulled himself out of fantasy. He was facing the inn's door. He opened it. There was a lamp on in the lobby. He was going to sit on Niaz's chair under the yellow colored and intense light, but he did not go inside the inn. He returned.

In the total darkness before dawn, he heard the sound of his footsteps so precisely that sometimes he felt he was the fine sand underfoot. He walked toward Parishan's platform. The silence was sprayed on Parishan's vacant place. Hedayat stopped breathing to hear better. There was the sound of a whisper, something like the nightingale sound. He passed by the light and turned toward the back of the inn, where he found the source of the sound. He saw Parishan, standing and facing the forest. He was motionlessness like a scarecrow and ceaselessly whispered under his lips, like the wind that blew to a wheat field.

Hedayat went ahead and stood beside the scarecrow. Parishan's voice slowly slipped onto space, "What do you see ahead, kid?"

What did the lad saw ahead? Nothing. The darkness! Only the branches of the nearest shrub that had scratched the night were barely visible. And a bit farther, there was a bright moving spot.

The lad, instead of replying the question, said, "I was in the middle of the inn, it was crowded. Then the thing broke, then the monster with a whip . . ."

Tears and choking did not allow him to speak. Parishan repeated under the lips several times, "The monster . . . monster . . . monster . . . . . you must break the monster's horn . . . it is somewhere near us. I smell their sacred fire. They are nearby."

The matchstick was struck and its flickering light fell on the face of the two. A deep red color appeared between the earth and the sky, "What do you want from the kid, maniac? Where should he go better than here?! What have you sniffed, Dervish?"

Faraz puffed at his cigarette and blew its smoke to Parishan's face.

Parishan did not turn his head, "I wish it was possible."

******

Obliso Travel Guide

"We are researchers. We love the desert and to chase the snakes and lizards, to take photos of them and do special things that are inexplicable and are boring to you. We are public servants."

When Niaz told Faraz that they needed a guide, Faraz stuck out his head from under the old blanket and asked, "They do not want a luggage carrier for free, do they? Where are these city guys headed to?!"

Niaz rested his head on the wall and avoided answering Faraz's question with an *I donno* look. Faraz returned to his euphoric nap again.

After a few minutes, Niaz said with a barely audible voice, "Even a donkey would not carry a load for free, bro! Obliso . . ."

Faraz jumped out from under the blanket like a spring and said, "What is their business there? Surely, they are looking for a treasure."

Niaz pursed his lips and said, "They said they would spend generously. God knows!"

Money is the common language of all people in the world. The task took a more serious shape and now Faraz - our happy-go-lucky Bushlambo - was sorting out how much they must pay to allow him to buy angel dust and weed and get rid of this hollow world. It was both fun and entertainment! Huh? What is better than that, the money and a trip.

"Why do not you take them yourself?" he asked.

"I guess I have a traveler coming my way," replied Niaz, which meant someone will come for sure.

They got out of the hideout together. Faraz leaped forward like a charging leopard, reached out and grasped the demonic boy's ear, "Where were you going bastard?"

The demonic boy was walking back toward their direction as he was caught. He was frightened. He groaned due to ear pain and his pale eyes showed traces of anger and fear. His lips did not move and he did not say anything. Like a terrified puppy, he struggled to free himself from Faraz's large hand.

Niaz asked carelessly, "Why are they interested in Obliso?"

In fact, he did not ask but was talking to himself.

Faraz was shouting, "You think I do not know you piss in my shoes, shithead! You cursed ominous one!"

A little later, the demonic boy ran to the plain. Faraz was in a conversation with the desert trekkers - or to put it more clearly - the research team.

*****

Part IV

Open Heart

A cloud on the horizon was extended to the eternity, like a white pigeon's wing with a shotgun pellet stuck in it. A red color was sprinkled to the sky, both on that endless soaring one, and the cloud patches that were moving away from the recent sun.

Niaz was restless. He could not sit on his usual boulder. He repeatedly put his cigarette on his lips, smoked it, and then went for the next one. The next cigarette and he could not calm down. (Is a traveler on his way?) Is it possible that Niaz's feeling goes wrong? He scratched his sweaty body and felt the need for someone beside him to chat with him. What to say? Well, it was obvious, about that strange feeling of the traveler's arrival. Someone who instructs him how to wipe the table to cleaned it up well, how to wipe the glass so that it does not get stained, about the fact that an innkeeper should not sleep at the wrong time, and should not be surprised by a traveler who comes in such a time that he is asleep and leaves in such a way that he could never imagine . . .

Our lad could have calmed him if he lent a sympathetic ear. He was not what Niaz had wished for at all. He was absent-minded. The painful thought that he had no talent in this area disturbed Niaz. But anyways, he thought to himself that he could make an innkeeper even from a wooden stick. But alas, Hedayat was not even a piece of wood.

Niaz left all of his agitation, thoughts, and unrest right there, and surrendered himself to the hideout. He released himself in smoke and euphoria. Seconds and minutes passed faster. It is a property of opium, it accelerates time. It allows the filled container to overflow. It overflows and you do not fear something might get wet down there. And you are not afraid. You allow the container to overflow and water covers the whole world.

Niaz's eyes were blood ridden. A humming sound circulated in his ears and his body was left to itself . . . everything was calm and silent, then, Hedayat's voice was heard, "Daddy Niaz . . . customer. .!"

The wire was thrown to the side and the straw and the poker were tossed to the other . . . The life-giving flame was abandoned and Niaz was no longer there. He had happily reached the coffee shop through the secret corridor. It was the black smeared coal miners' day. A mine that nobody knew where it was. They arrived with two Russian *Ije* motorcycles. They leaned against the table in the middle of the coffee shop. They looked at each other with inquiring eyes - which shone like a lamp in the dark on their black faces. They gestured to Niaz - who paced around them like a wandering ghost - without saying a word, and Niaz realized they wanted tea and a hookah. They were customers, and it cheered up Niaz.

*****

The Appearance

While Faraz at this side of the coffee shop - high and happy of the victory - was talking about sand and sky and gray bones under the *Dragon Slayer* hill, on the other side, Niaz placed the cups in a tray with a barista's special skill and then rotated it. He had fixed his gaze on black smeared guests, and his beloved Hedayat awkwardly carried the precious jar for the customers who were sitting around the table, under *Uncle Hookah*'s painting.

Our poor Dervish - that man who was free of the bounds of time and place - did not care if anyone was a coffee shop's customer or a guest of the inn, or that the gray bones, as Faraz claimed, were hundreds of years old and the remnants of the last dragon; and thousands of other important things in the world. At that time, and in the midst of arrivals and departures and at the center of the pleasant commotion and agitation of others, he experienced an awful dread. It was as if behind his blank eyes - behind those holes hidden under his hair - he had two shiny blue eyes and with those two naked eyes, he saw the farthest of farthest. He saw something that you and I, a scientist, an architect, a businessman, and a baker and a farmer could not see.

Faraz had jumped off the Jeep and picked up a handful of dirt from the ground and said to the four desert trekkers with a confident and professional tone, "Do you believe that we are from this earth too, there is a long way between my stiff and filthy flesh and your white and soft flesh and this worthless damned soil?"

And Obliso watched them from inside of its darkness, and the four desert trekkers had sensed that captivating and scary gaze all too well.

Obliso is, in fact, a rocky mountain with two summits at the same height, two heads with a large body. At the bottom of it, there is a gap at a height of 10 meters and a width that allowed a camel caravan - that had lost its way in the ancient world - to pass through. An upside down valley. A passageway with a limestone ceiling connecting the world on this side to the world beyond Obliso.

Niaz asked his black smeared coalmining and tired customers, "What mine, where?"

And his customers said nothing except that it was far and hard to find!

But Hedayat . . .

On the way to reach the four unknown and anonymous people, Hedayat's foot stumbled over something. The corner of the rolled up old rug . . . he, the precious glass jar, Niaz's mesmerizing eyes, all floated in the air. The sound of breaking something and the *thump* of Hedayat's falling down and Niaz's short *much* mixed together and all of it merged with the short tinkling of the bell and then, the long creak of the opening door. A tall figure, a heavy and magnificent shadow, appeared in the coffee shop's doorway.

****

Niaz's Show

(He is in the coffee shop)

The jar's crystalline fragments were scattered and spun around themselves like spinning top. Light beams fell on the wall by reflecting on each particle.

An aghast, desperate and hopeless, Niaz looked at the pieces and shards of one of his loved ones that were dancing now in the midst of the world's uproar.

- "Not a big deal!"

The stranger man stepped forward with his long, triangular-snouted shoes. The jar's fragments crackled under his feet, and he walked and approached like a vast and calm river. With the left hand, he picked up the lad like a kitten and a moment later, lowered him so he could stand on two legs on the floor. As Hedayat's feet touched the floor, he turned around and remembered something. Something shadowy and far away. A phantom of reality. A vague color of the truth that was sprayed in the air. Niaz suddenly came to himself, "A traveler, a guest!"

He moved his stiff jaw and the tongue that was broken in its mouth, "Welcome sir, at your service . . ."

A guest had come who was different than the rest. From the black smeared coalminer jerks who smoked hookah at the table and sipped the tea. He was different than the groaning and tired farmers who said, 'The goddamn has have dried up'. He was even different than those desert trekkers who listened to fantasies that Faraz had made up hoping to get a fistful of cash out of it.

The stranger seemed to know every corner of the inn by heart. He pointed his index finger to the wall, and then raised his eyebrows, which meant Niaz's old chair is there. Then, he pointed his finger to another direction and raised his eyebrows again, which meant the room number 4 was there . . .

Then, he turned the chair that was on the left of *Uncle Hookah* to face the wall and sat down on it. He pulled out a cigarette out of his golden metallic cigarette box. He stroked a matchstick and in the midst of smoke opened his two arms toward the wall and said, "There was a big tapestry! Rostam, Sohrab . . . where is the Shahnameh tapestry?"

Niaz's Shahnameh tapestry! Amazing!

With that statement, blood began to run through Niaz's veins like a horse. He was breathless by delight and was going to pass out by excitement, and he stammered with difficulty, "It is their sir! It is! Somewhere around here . . . God knows I put it aside so that an appreciative person would remember it."

Then, unwittingly and without any apparent reason, he hugged Hedayat and mumbled deliriously a few times, "It was not a big deal, who cares . . . it did not matter, it was not important."

"So, where is the innkeeper?" asked the uninvited guest.

Niaz bent down in front of the man and said, "He is right here, right here," and put his hand on his chest, "Here . . ."

He rushed to the hideout. A short door to the corridor from the samovar and cups' chamber, from the corridor to his secret territory . . . the den's door opened. He disappeared into the hideout's closet and threw something like a rolled-up rug on his shoulder like a gun, and went back all the way.

He was confused. He felt a hangover. He panted and sweat ran down his forehead. A naïve and adorable Niaz was cheered up like a child who has been given a balloon or a puppy.

With Hedayat's assistance, he hung his Shahnameh tapestry on the coffee shop wall. He clumsily threw a few chairs that were in front of the tapestry to the side. During that time, the stranger did not move from his place. He did not even scratch his neck or smooth out the wrinkles on his pants.

The stage was ready.

Niaz looked at his meaty and aged hands . . . something was missing. He glanced questioningly at Hedayat, "Is not something missing dear? I guess something is missing."

Faraz shouted from behind all those who were bedazzled in the midst of the hubbub, "Old man . . . the wand, where is your storytelling wand?"

Niaz jumped out of the coffee shop and went behind the inn, heading for the forest, 'Perhaps that sole enthusiastic guy is not interested anymore. Maybe when I put the wand on Rostam's two-pronged beard, he would say no, I am not in the mood now . . . "

He was teetering and looking for a good wooden stick on the ground. No, this one is skewed, this . . . no! No! It is too short. That one is wide and heavy.

- "The storytelling wand must be bright and compact, not too short, not too long, a wand to stick it under my armpit, slap my palms together and read the Shahnameh. A stick like . . . like this stick . . .”

A stylish, slim, compact and nice colored twig caught his eyes. He raised his head and the ominous and unwelcome face of the demonic boy with that ugly smile showed up. He had grabbed the stick and stood up against Niaz.

“That's a good boy, lend me the stick,” said Niaz with sweet talk and a fake-sympathetic voice.

The demonic boy looked at the stick. He glanced at Niaz. Again, he looked at the stick. He looked at Niaz, “It is *my* stick . . .”

“Yeah, *your* stick. Just lend it to me . . .” replied Niaz seductively.

The demonic boy looked at the stick again. As he was going to shift his eyes toward Niaz, the world went black. Niaz's five fingers grasped his disgusting yellow face. The stick was under Niaz's armpit and he hastily ran to the coffee shop. The demonic boy coiled up on the hot soil.

Now everything was alright. Niaz felt like he was forty years old at that moment.

The world has returned to the good old days. The storytelling was rewarding again. The coffee shop crowd's gaze was fixed on Niaz's stylish wand and narrating lips.

The newly arrived guest took off his hat and put it on his knees. A mysterious smile crawled on his lips.

Niaz was ready, ready to narrate.

Everything was now in place. Niaz in the center of the show, the four miners had faced the Shahnameh tapestry, and the four desert trekkers at the end of the coffee shop were concentrated on the tapestry. Faraz was there too. Mr.

Hedayat, sitting next to the enthusiastic stranger, stared at the scene. He had never seen the tapestry so beautiful and magnificent.

Suddenly . . . he remembered something that shook him from head to toe . . . it was so familiar? The tapestry . . . the shattered jar . . . that guy, the ambient noise . . .

Niaz rubbed his palms together, raised the wand and put it on Rostam's beard:

When the bright sun from high heavens
Was going to throw the shining lasso
On Rostam's arm was a bead
And that bead was well-known around the world
He gave it to her and said, "Keep it."
If fate gives you a daughter
Pick it and fix it to her hair
For good luck and worldwide fortune
But if the horoscope is cast to give you a son
Tie it to his arm as a sign of the father

Sohrab and was passing away in Rostam's lap. This is the end of their story. Sohrab sniffed the smell of death and Rostam shed tears. The tapestry paintings were typically unconscious artwork. Raw and amateurish drawings. Rostam's face had faded out but his two-pronged beard was still intact. Sohrab had faded out from the waist down. But his eyes sparkled. On the right side of the tapestry, there was a young woman with a cow on her shoulder, stepping down the staircase of a royal building. A long red skirt covered her lower limbs and she had a green shirt on.

Below the image of the cow-carrying woman, the demon was trapped in Rostam's lasso. Behind it, Rostam and Rakhsh were standing side by side and farther away, a deer was drinking water from the river. On the left side of the tapestry, Zal had a newborn baby in his arms while sitting on a royal throne, and Roudabe stood beside him happily and cheerfully . . . There was a phrase below each image written in black, *The Third Phase, Slaying the Dragon.* Another place, the word *Zal* was written in white. *The Second Phase, Passing Through the Dry Desert . . . The Witch . . . The Seventh Phase, Fighting the Albedo Demon!* The lasso of their looks was undoubtedly tied to the point where Niaz's wand rested. Right on the Rostam's beard. Niaz's great grief, deep sadness, and regretfulness . . .

As he opened the armor and saw that bead
He tore off all of his clothes
He repeatedly said, "O' you who were killed by my hand,
Brave and praiseworthy in any forum."
He ceaselessly shed blood and tore out hair
His head was covered with dirt and his face was covered with water.

*****

The Second Battle
(Parishan and the Stranger Man)

Niaz's performance was awesome. At times, he tripped but did not fall. Sometimes his hand trembled, but he did not let go of the wand! Like an agile dancer waved his wand on stage. Like a skilled vocal performer, he raised the voice where it should be raised and lowered it down where it was needed, and mislead his audience with dazzling wordplay. He was forty. He found another Niaz inside himself. There was a twinkle in his eyes.

He had the new guest in mind throughout the twists and turns of the narration. All his efforts were to please the tall and magnificent man. He took Sohrab to the Rostam's arms and took Rostam to the end of the wishes. He gathered all of the people of the story around himself and read the poem the way that it was meant to be read.

Large and cold drops of sweat ran down Niaz's forehead and spine. 'I have a hangover?' The fear of a hangover engulfed him and shook him. How on earth could he leave the guest and crawl into the den? The stone of a voice broke the Niaz's glass of thoughts. The voice tossed a word to everyone with full force, "Asij. .!"

Niaz's new guest pulled back his right leg that he had crossed on his left leg. He got up from the chair and walked a few steps toward the door. Over there, at the coffee shop's doorframe, a figure stood withdrawn into himself. He had a book in his arms and a stick in his hand. He was Parishan! That event was if we cannot exactly say unprecedented, but an unusual event that Parishan walk into the coffee shop.

As if any warm and bright place and any relief and rest were forbidden to him. The newly arrived guest smiled at Parishan and said, "You are here Dervish! I have come to see you . . . comrade."

He extended his hand toward Parishan as if he was going to ask for something. Parishan pressed the book to his bosom. He stepped forward limping and feeling his way, in a very weak and tired manner. He stood in front of the man. His lips moved to find a word, but seemingly he did not find anything. He found nothing!

*****

Asij

Asij was a seeker, seeking a valuable treasure. By sniffing a valuable treasure, he had walked many paths and passed many mountains to reach this place from the other side of the woods and the deserts. His past and Parishan's past were tied together at a dark point. The past that hid secrets in its heart like the earth and kept them away from prying eyes like a chest.

He wore a black hat. A cylinder 8 to 10 inches tall with nice golden decorations. The top of the hat was wider than the bottom. He was tall. He walked slowly, but he was agile. His face was burned by the solar radiation that shone on it most of the day. But his skin still sparkled and his eyes were bright.

He and Parishan were sitting facing each other beside the unreliable pole that was the Dervish's stronghold and was slowly chattering in a heated and vital conversation:

- "Mr. crazy Dervish. Is it not ridiculous? The most important thing is in your custody but what use? The blind get the best eye candy, the sweetest sounds fall on deaf ears, and the most sweet-smelling flower comes to the hands of someone who is in the waste and sewage business. Parishan's face deformed with the Asij's words. His nose shook. In the hollow of his eyes, he felt an unpleasant sensation and his mouth sensed an annoying bitter taste. Asij was still talking.

The dervish man stared sourly and bitterly at Asij (having turned the two empty holes toward the sound) and was grunting. If he found the power of knocking down Asij in himself, he would have certainly done it.

- "Wherever you go, devastation follows. I heard from the wind. From the mountains. I hear from the ground. They have told me. You bring fire to this place. You are the destruction itself."

Asij's eyes shifted. The fire inside his eyes flamed up. He got up and walked back two steps. He turned and returned to Parishan again. He stood straight up in front of Parishan who was on the ground, smoothed out the crease on his coat, and then he put his hand on the badge on his chest (a silvery fire and a black tree image with four branches in the heart of the fire).

- "Fire cleanses. Fire warms up the cold nights of those stopped in their tracks. The stronghold of lost people against predators . . . life . . ."

Parishan interrupted Asij's speech and asked, "You came here to look for what?"

Asij was glad that Parishan raised the main point. He bent his body so that his lips get near Dervish's ear lest a stranger hear him.

- "To be honest, I did not want to say it to you so soon . . . that is, abruptly and hurriedly. But, well, since your presence at this location is not accidental, just like me, I thought to myself that my old friend could help me at a risky and important moment such as now," he moved his lips closer to Dervish's ear and said quietly, "I must tell my dear Dervish that I want the treasure."

"Go back the way you came!" replied Parishan.

- "You stubborn and ignorant Dervish! They are up and running. Now that I am talking to you pigheaded guy, they have reached here! Both Combatants and Devotees. Are not these names familiar? They are under our nose, looking for the treasure. You know them, crazy Dervish . . . they are cruel. They have an ideology. They have a goal. Nothing is more horrific than men and women who have a sacred cause. I will take the treasure with me before their dirty hands touch it."

Parishan pressed the book hard to his bosom.

*****

Fire in the Reed Bed

Niyaz gave room 4 to the new guest. The last room. The room that if you got out of it and turned to the right and walked to the end of the hallway, you could hear the howling of the wind from the broken glass of its small hatch, and if you were curious and looked out, you could see the short shrubs and behind them - farther away - the hills and the mountains.

Asij came out of the room and went to the stairs. The sound of a conversation came from the other room. He stopped a few moments and cocked an ear. He could not get it. He went down the stairs. Niyaz was napping on his royal chair.

- "I was there, right where you stand, the trees on the back were healthier, there was always a showmanship stage in front of the inn, entertainments that made you feel good. Anyone standing there and stares out must do something.

Niyaz was kicked out of the sweet euphoric nap to reality. He looked at Asij.

The lad was standing in front of the window, under the gloomy inn ceiling, in the old plain's cavity. Asij took a few steps towards him.

"Time is out, the risk is near and there is little hope. So, listen to my dear boy," and continued, "What do you see outside? Are you thinking of those dust and winds? No! Obviously not! There is not such a thing in those eyes. You look at the moon. The dark patch of the moon. But you do not think about the moon either. Well, then, about what . . ."

Hedayat shifted his deep eyes from Asij's face and fixed them again on the moon crescent.

What did he think about?

- "Yes, yes, smart boy. The moon! The inaccessible moon . . . one must start out sooner to reach the moon!

A few more steps . . . and he put a hand on the boy's shoulder. The heat of Asij's hand ran from the lad's thin shirt to his skin. From skin to flesh. From flesh to veins. From veins to his blood, and set his soul ablaze.

****

Sickle and Rifle

As Asij was talking to Hedayat in the Null Zone at the most sensitive moment, the two male and two female desert trekkers had a meeting in room 3 upstairs. The skinny young man with short curly hair pulled out a large roll of paper from his khaki backpack. He opened it and spread it between the two beds on a corroded metal cupboard. The man with afro hairstyle and the woman (the woman who gave Hedayat the gift) were sitting on a bed, and the other man and woman were on the opposite bed. For a while, all four looked at the large paper in silence which was seemingly a map, until one of the women said: "Well . . . !"

The man with curly hair said, "You mean it is here?"

"Yes . . ." replied the man and woman on the opposite bed at the same time.

The sheet spread on the cupboard was a map with scribbled text. A red logo on the top of the sheet was the only clear and recognizable thing on it. A five-pointed star at the top, below it a crossed sickle and rifle, on the right a grape of wheat, and on the left a slanted line with two short lines across it.

******

The Third Battle

(Asij and Niyaz)

Asij said quietly in the lad's ear, "It is like emerging wings on a caterpillar. The caterpillar transforms into a butterfly. Nobody calls it a caterpillar anymore, but calls it a butterfly."

Like any other child of that age, the strongest power in Hedayat's mind started to roll, the power of imagination! He saw himself as a caterpillar. His back split and from beneath his shell, two wings with the color of daddy Niyaz's Shahnameh cover sprung up.

The stunned and confused old Niyaz could not move from his place, as if his hands and ankles were in locks and chains. In front of his unbelieving eyes, that dude with his wonderful speech was gradually kidnapping the lad. He told him to grow wings and fly from here and go to the moon!

- "What crap!"

Asij said that out there, in faraway places, there were things that might make Hedayat to grow horns or scream of delight! Such language did not please the sick old man at all. Hedayat was a godsend angel to run the inn after Niyaz, was not he? This beautiful inn, which has been standing for ages by the side of the legendary Silk Road with glory and honor. Who was going to go down the path if Hedayat was not there? Who will reinforce the wooden beam under the coffee shop ceiling?

- "So what is this nonsense?"

Niyaz removed the magical and invisible locks and chains from his hands and ankles. He stamped the shackles' spell underfoot and pulled himself away from the chair. He teetered forward and grabbed the back of Asij's collar, "What are these ridiculous things you feed to the child, Diablo?"

Asij turned angrily and stared at Niyaz. The confrontation of the two was the great inequality of nature. Asij was taller than Niyaz by a full head and neck.

Even with this remarkable superiority, the old man was not discouraged and continued, "Ha! Ha!. Who do you think you are? A king or vizier?"

Asij looked down at Niyaz from above. He brought his face forward, so close that he could sense Niyaz's rapid breathing on his chin; A cold and tired breath. He said with a confident and careless tone, "Dear sir! When did you kidnap this kid and bring him here to serve you and your stupid guests? What heinous cruelty!"

Niyaz stammered with obvious fear, "Kidnap? What do you mean by kidnap, sir? What the hell! One cannot kidnap his own child, can he?"

Short bursts of nervous laughter did not allow him to talk normally, he added with great difficulty, "What . . . What . . . is the plan in your head, sir . . . what are you looking for?
"

Asij slowly and indifferently looked around the inn. His eyes turned around and around and around and finally locked on Hedayat. Niyaz wanted to swallow his saliva, but his mouth was dry, totally dry. Dry like the sea.

Asij removed his hat and said, "Nothing, my dear Mr. Niyaz, nothing. Everything is yours . . . except . . . my treasure."

- "Your treasure?" (Niyaz smirked) "Your treasure is not in my possession, sir. Here, we only have tea and eggs and Dooqh (yogurt and water) and butter . . . we serve such stuff. These are our treasures."

A spark lit at the back of Niyaz's mind, Parishan's holy book!

Asij took a few steps toward Hedayat (The lad was struggling in immense indecisiveness and his mind was shattered to a thousand pieces.)

- "For your information, sir, the honorable Mr. Niyaz, owner of this beautiful inn and at the service of travelers and those stuck in the road, do you have any idea what is the sentence for kidnapping a child and hiding him - for many years, for that matter.

- "Kidnapping? What kidnapping? This kid is my real son."

Asij asked, "You mean you did not abduct this kid and hide him for many years?"

- "He came on his own . . ."

Niyaz collapsed. A dam that cracked and then collapsed. The flood of tears and helplessness erupted from his very being . . . he collapsed.

*****

Eyes in the Dark

Behind the inn, after the flat ground, behind the shrubs, a few pairs of eyes were peeping the inn in the dark.

One asked quietly, "Is it not time, brother?"

"I do not know; I do not know. Hopefully, the news will arrive tonight," replied the other.

The first voice again asked, "So, who will tell us?"
- "The one who must break the news!"
- "How are they going to tell us in the middle of this desert, bro?"
- "The news will arrive tonight."
Those who had hidden behind the shrubs in the dark of the night were the black smeared men. Niyaz's coffee shop customers. Those who had introduced themselves as miners.

****

One of the Paradises on Earth

Asij threatened Niyaz with police, trial, and imprisonment too. The old man, who felt fear in every cell in his body, lost the game at that moment.
He whispered to himself, "God gave him to me, did not He? Is it not ridiculous?"
He sat on the inherited chair with a shaky body. The invisible chains and locks wrapped around his hands and ankles again and tied him up like a defeated monster.
Asij, relieved from the old man's claim of possession over the boy, returned to Hedayat again. Now, one of the rivals was taken out, 'What should I do with the crazy Dervish?"
He had to make Hedayat fascinated and devoted, otherwise he could not separate him from the land that he was accustomed to, just based on bare and cold facts. Asij continued tempting him by talking about big cities with tall towers. Beautiful wooden bridges over clear rivers. Endless stairs that reach the sky.

Over there, people's clothes were colorful and beautiful garments. Those people had nothing in common with the dumb folk in that area. Asij showed Paradise to Hedayat.

******

Asij's Great Treasure

Asij had found the treasure.

Treasure? What treasure?

The treasure is in the inn. For many years, that treasure entered the coffee shop via its secret door. Picked a piece of cloth and wiped the tables one by one.

It removed the dust from *Uncle Hookah*'s mustache and eyes and hat. Smoothed out the corner of the carpet that was rolled up. If shards of glass were thrown at the corners, it collected them. It swept every inch of the coffee shop with great care and prepared everything for the arrival of guests.

Niyaz had taught and indoctrinated Hedayat to do those tasks in such a way that the child thought every day a large number of guests - amounting to China's population - would come there.

Asij raised his voice (if one could draw it or take a photo of the sound, Asij's voice was now like a young sharp mountain and compared to that, Hedayat looked like a frightened and lost fawn).

- "Behind those mountains, there is a path that passes through the mountain. After that, we will come to one of the most beautiful things on earth. You will not believe what you will see."

He quietly whispered in Hedayat's ear, "It is worth seeing!"

Asij's voice resembled a seductive mermaid's. He wanted to lure Hedayat into the water of knowledge with seduction and flirting and charm.

"However, we're not supposed to stay there forever," Asij stared at the ceiling, stretched out his arms and drew things in the air, "There are even better things," he looked around with suspicion, "We just have to get going, dear boy," he raised his voice a little, "If Lord Niyaz issues the permission."

Niyaz was motionless and looked ahead with frustrated eyes. The invisible chains and locks were pressing him so hard to the hereditary chair that it gradually felt like rubble and pebble in the shoe.

Asij got ready to go. He said something in the lad's ear. He felt a deep joy within him. Like a thin light in a compelling night. While he was moving away from the boy, he blinked at him wickedly.

Hedayat laughed.

****

Mobarezin (Fighters) *vs.* Fadaeez (Devotees)

The curly-haired man picked up the map from the closet, rolled it up and put it in his backpack. The woman who sat beside him with large eyes and elongated face said: "Comrade Keyvan! We do not get anything more from this scrap of paper. We can waste time here till the whole world gets the news."

78

The man (Keyvan) said asked, "Those four suckers at the coffee shop . . . who were they? They showed up exactly when we arrived. I asked the innkeeper. They did not come here before. Is it not suspicious?!"

"That nasty dwarf looks very familiar to me . . ." remarked the woman.

The bed creaked with their every move. The shimmering flame of the kerosene lamp alternately and eerily cast their shorter and longer shadows on the wall. The other woman had gazed at the shadows and eventually, the spell of the shadows hypnotized her and took her to dreamland.

The other man said with his very thin and feminine voice, "All is ok, this, this, this is the right location, Obliso, the sparse forest, the i, i, inn. Ok . . ."

The first woman continued, "Well, we are near the target, now we know what we are looking for. But our problem is that it is not a suitcase to stick it under the armpit and flee, or a piece of paper to tie in and put in our pocket."

The wind intensified and through the broken window pane, its howling sound echoed in the hallway and shook the doors.

The other woman who was still silent shuddered and said: "Look, comrade! My hands are shaking. in my opinion, we would better finish it sooner and return home. I am getting sick in this dirt and filth."

The sound of something falling scared everyone. Then, a huge shock shook the walls and the ground and the wind twisted around the four corners of the inn. It grabbed the inn's feet like a diabolic hand and pulled on it.

****

The Crazy Wind Talks to a Person as Such

Faraz, Niyaz, Asij and Hedayat all stood looking down at Parishan. The Dervish was still shaking. He was busy saying a prayer and telling beads when suddenly his support collapsed. The wooden pole gave way under both his weight and the upstairs protrusion. It collapsed with a terrible sound and sank in the sand. Niyaz was condoling Parishan with a trembling and mumbling voice, and in fact, he was condoling his own heart. Asij picked up Parishan's book, which had been thrown to a corner and looked it over. He wet his thumb with saliva and rubbed it on its leather cover. He tried to read the text on it under the flickering light of the light bulb. Parishan frantically called for the book and blindly felt around to find it. Asij returned the book to him and whispered sadly, "Where are those great days of glory and pride? Where did they you go, Dervish? Where did they rob you of that thing?"

Now, the resemblance of the two was obvious. Their voices were very similar, and their speech as well, the tone and dialect of the voice. If Parishan had not been so withdrawn and collapsed into himself, he was the same height as Asij. If his face had not been exposed to the sand and dirt, the hot sun and the cold dry winter temperatures for years, it was very much like Asij's handsome face. What was the secret of that similitude . . . The wind pounded hard on the inn's wall? One could reasonably imagine that everything would collapse at any moment.

Parishan withdrew into himself more than before. Niyaz said a prayer under his breath and repeated every second, "May God have mercy on us! I apologize to god . . ."

Asij was restless as if there was a connection between the stubborn restless wind and his inner world. He paced back and forth along the length of the wooden bench in front of the inn. As he walked to and fro for the last time, he suddenly found himself alone in front of the inn's door, facing an old woman who was gazing at him.

Asij removed his hat and told the old woman, "Everyone has a fate, Maahrokh. Everyone has to go in his own way. Sometimes this road may pass over our fantasies and destroy them all."

"No one can do anything," the old woman whispered quietly, "We cannot make it either."

****

Part V

The Bridge

Hedayat was shaken out of his sleep by a heavy hand. In the small shimmering flame, he recognized Asij's face. He closed his eyes and went to sleep again.

- ". . . ready?"

Hedayat was standing on the bridge between sleep and wakefulness; a scary stone bridge with dark water flowing underneath. Everywhere was grayish. In the surroundings, blue steam raised to the air.

A shapeless figure appeared in front of Hedayat. A light opened its way in the midst of the formless and black mass. A large hand came out of the light and pointed to him . . .

- "Hedayat . . . Hedayat . . ."

Hedayat gently extended his arm toward the big hand. His fingers interlaced with the large hand's fingers. His hand slowly spread out like steam and was drawn into the formless mass.

Hedayat!!!

The lad jumped from his sleep. Asij's face was in front of him. He was sweaty and his hair was sticking to his forehead and he panted.

- "It is getting late . . . we have to go!"

****

In the Middle of the Evil Circle
- "The little boy? What little boy? The one in the coffee shop?"
Samad, the head of the group of four had brought important news to the three other beasts. The news was scribbled badly on a piece of paper that was torn carelessly out of a notebook:
"Hello there. Thankfully, you have found the treasure. The lad who works in the coffee shop, the innkeeper's stepson, is called Hedayat. Bring the boy here immediately."
All four fake miners jumped out from behind the hills. They attacked the inn like barbarians, waving ax and knife. They got there fast. As they passed by Parishan, he snored and shut up again. The light bulb above Dervish's head was off unlike other times.
They passed the entrance to the coffee shop, kicked and broke the door to Niyaz's house and entered one after the other.
The old man and the old woman were standing at a corner. The old woman had pulled the blanket over her and shook. Niyaz looked frightened too. Interestingly, the fake desert trekkers were there as well. All four had covered their faces with cloth and scarves and were standing alert at the four corners of the room.
- "Hold up your hands in the name of the party. Who are you jerks?"
One of the fake desert trekkers threatened the four fake miners with the Colt in his hand.
The sound of falling axes and knives was a sign of the surrender of miners.

- "Well, we are miners!"
- "The bullish miners! Do you dig with ax and sword? Perhaps you are looking for coal here too?! Huh?"
"Where is the lad?" yelled the fake miners' boss.
One of the women stepped forward and stared into his foolish face. Samad stood on his toes to avoid being seen shorter than a woman!
- "This is Chubby Samad. Chubby Samad, are you looking for the kid here?.. Why?"
Samad, as he had reached up as much as he could, replied: "Yes, I am boss Samad!"
Then, as if the fake desert trekkers suddenly remembered Hedayat, they rushed to the door like madmen. The fake miners were pushed to the side. Samad got up from the ground with difficulty and groaned under his breath, "The bitch calls me a dwarf, we will see . . ."
There was the sound of laughter and Samad turned red and shouted, "Who was it, who, say it if you dare so that I pull your tongue out of your mouth?"

****

The Escape

Twenty minutes before the foolish and filthy brothers (the fake miners) attack the inn, and before the evil comrades (those four fake desert trekkers) run down to Niyaz's house from their rooms; in the dark, a shadow opened the door to Niyaz's house and crawled in like a fairy. When he left the house, a small shadow was with him. They slowly walked toward the coffee shop.

Asij stopped as he passed by Parishan's light. He looked at Parishan's vacant place.

- "Where is he?"

He stood under the light bulb. He stretched his long arms toward the light bulb and turned it. It became dark.

- "Asij, is it your brother?"

Dervish came out from behind the wall. He took several steps with great effort and with the help of the wall. He stood in the narrow twilight strip. He had become feebler than ever. Slimmer, more crippled and hapless. Asij approached Parishan as he held Hedayat's tiny hand. He was in doubt. He did not know what would be Hedayat's reaction.

"It is me, brother, I have to finish the job, and" he replied quietly, "Time is out."

Dervish teetered closer, he looked lonelier than ever, "The human being, this scroll of pain and suffering, where is that great relief. Where is it?"

"Where it is supposed to be," replied Asij hastily.

Dervish turned his head to the sky, "Why did you leave me alone?"

His shoulders began to shake and he was hollowed out. His was breathless. He pulled out the book from under the old cotton cloth and held it in Hedayat's direction. Hedayat extended his hand but Asij stopped him. He took the book and said, "Let me keep it, rest assured Parishan, rest assured brother."

In the tiny light that was in Asij's hand, Hedayat could see the face of both. Parishan's eyes should be similar to Asij's. It should have the same steady look.

Dervish grabbed Hedayat's hand and pulled him closer and hugged him tightly. He sniffed Hedayat, said a statement, and he goes, "Please, I beg, please . . . the book, take care of the book."

Then he stepped back and slowly went away.

His was facing Asij and Hedayat as he disappeared into the darkness.

. . .

The coffee shop's door opened. Asij held up the flame so that all of the space would be lit. They went to the chamber at the end of the coffee shop. They stepped inside. They went through the secret door and entered the hallway. Hedayat did not know how Asij was so familiar with that route. They entered Niyaz's den. Asij went to the closet and with a wide smile on his lips, forcefully pulled out the large chest with great effort. He moved the old rug to the side and pulled out a chip-ax from the bag he carried along. He stroked at the ground a few times. Then he began to dig slowly. The underlying cement was brittle and fragile and shattered after a few strokes. Asij threw away the broken pieces quickly and began to clean it with two hands.

Gradually, the metal parts showed up. After he pushed aside all of the cement, a metal hatch appeared. Asij kicked it a couple of times, then took the knob and began to pull. The hatch opened with a muffled sound. The sound of opening a can!

The hatch was completely open. Asij turned his flashlight on and large stone stairs appeared in the light. A gentle and clear fear engulfed Hedayat. He remembered a lot of things; daddy Niyaz, the mother, the demonic boy, his dear uncle, the inn, the sunset scope from the window . . . and last but not least, Parishan!

All those years paraded before his eyes, like fast forwarding a movie, like a Déjà vu perfume. Asij smiled and sat half raised on the ground in a special pose. He raised the right knee and hugged it. He looked up and narrowed his eyes and said to an unseen personality, "This one is mine!"

****

Faraz's Critical Situation

When the false desert trekkers followed by the fake miners, stormed poor Niyaz's house, Faraz was lying on the coffee shop's roof and partially saw and heard the ruckus. He was very worried. He was concerned about his brother, his brother's wife, Hedayat, Asij, and Parishan . . . his pride did not allow him to hide up there like the cowards, and on the other hand, he had to fix something important . . . He stared at the den and whispered under his breath, "We must make it!"

******

Lamentation

As the noise diminished and the sound of the miners' motorcycles and the roar of desert trekkers' Jeep faded out, Faraz jumped down cautiously. He passed by the Dervish's vacant place and walked to his brother's house. He did not know what a disaster was awaiting him. There was the sound of Niyaz and Maahrokh crying and groaning. Faraz opened the door and went inside. The old man and the old woman had hugged each other and wept loudly. Faraz hugged them both and listened to Niyaz's lamentation:
- "The kid was daddy's breath . . . the kid was daddy's eyes . . . the kid was daddy's walking stick . . ."
Faraz thought about all those he had lost. He thought to himself, "This was not the first one, this will not be the last one?"

****

The Occult Land

And I said [joyfully]:
Be careful, god, he is winning!
The sun is setting and the night comes.
That train is frozen in time,
Oh god, he is winning!
Hedayat and Asij breezed through the stairs as if they were entering a cave opening. The stairs were made of large stone slabs and the size and distance of the slabs was consistent, which was a telltale of a competent architect and builder. Asij had to bend down slightly. However, farther down the mysterious tunnel, it was wider and more

beautiful. Sometimes, they reached a dead-end with just a weird gap on its right or left. A narrow gap that one could easily miss if one would not look carefully. They went through it and another tunnel began with plenty of tight and narrow entrances. The more they went down, the more beautiful and magnificent their surroundings looked. They were going through a labyrinth that could never be negotiated without Asij. All passageways had a slight downward slope. Sometimes they reached stone steps and sometimes a huge empty cavern that was the shape of an extruded circle, and a good breeze stroked their faces from its top part. It was a kind of special architecture that was gradually revealing itself. They continued walking till they reached a flat and spacious place with a high roof like an underground Earth!

Hedayat was surprised as Asij pointed the flashlight to the surroundings; a city! Yes, a city with plenty of rooms, narrow corridors, a large square, enormous stone platforms, and beautiful stone statues. A large fish that wrapped itself around a big tree. A man with a long and twisted beard, with one hand, pointed upwards and his other hand pointed down. Stylish and racy goddesses. The statutes were all carved out of stone; beautiful, integrated and precise!

Asij sat on a platform. The platforms encircled a pool. The tree and fish statute was in the middle of the dock pool. Hedayat sat on another platform and enjoyed the amazing world around him.

Asij spoke after a long quick walk in silence, "It is beautiful, is not it, dear boy? As I said, we have other beautiful things ahead . . ."

Asij got up. He threw his head down and slowly went around the large statute. Hedayat's head and eyes followed the circular path that Asij walked. Then Asij went to one of the rooms. He came out and lit the torches fixed to the walls of that city one by one. The light increased by the moment and enhanced the beauty of that place as well. At every corner, on top of the hefty pillars, column capitals were carved out of stone. Indeed, that place was much more beautiful than Hedayat could ever imagine.

They spent an hour to chill out. Asij lay on the platform with one eye open and closed the other eye! However, Hedayat went from room to room with agitation and fascination. He walked on nicely colored stones and was immersed in amazement of all of that beauty.

Asij warned, "Do not get too far prince. Down here, nothing is easier than getting lost!"

"What is this place?" asked Hedayat.

Asij replied with a historian's tone of voice, "Those who have built this city had a goal. To escape from the enemy and survive to forbid and heavy magic spells. There must have been a terrible thing out there that forced them to get down here . . . I do not know exactly what. We restored everything when we found this place. It became our temple, our pagoda."

What did Asij mean by "us"? This underground city was the reminder of an age of fear in the heart of one of the glorious empires. A two thousand and so years old relic.

Who were those people who accompanied Asij on special days to sweep, hold rituals, dust the statues and monuments? What was the purpose of their gathering here? What were they seeking? What was their occupation? Why did not they tell anyone about this city?

Asij issued the order to move. The two travel buddies extinguished all lights and entered a room. From that room, they entered another large corridor through a secret door and continued their way.

They reached the end of the large corridor and got out of the city limits. Asij chose a path among dozens of other paths. He did not think about it as if he had walked that way many times and lived in this mysterious underground city. As if it was his home town. A vast cavern with nice statutes and well-decorated hallways ended at a narrow tunnel again. Then they reached the stairs. They climbed the large stone staircase.

Asij was thinking about Faraz.

****

Tragedy and Victory

While Asij and Hedayat were walking the underground pathway far from the eyes of others, the two comrades and four brothers with a Jeep and a motorcycle were looking for someone behind the forest that they guessed must be Hedayat. They found him mutilating the dead lizard's corpse in the woods. He escaped as he saw them and got out of the forest. Although he was limping and had a poor posture, he could run faster than a deer. It seemed he had been fleeing all his life by nature. He ran to Obliso followed by the Jeep and two motorcycles. They hit the sand dunes and jumped over them. The dust that had risen to the air made the landscape look like a battlefield. Just when the chasers thought they had won the easy game, the target disappeared suddenly . . .

The demonic boy returned to the place where he was ready. In a daring free fall, he dived into a deep well like a swimming champion.

On the other side, two members of the Mobarezin (The Fighters) team (a male and a female) discovered Niaz's hideout. They messed it up, broke and overturned all of Niaz's hidden assets and kicked and smashed his brass brazier. They removed the mirror from the wall and smashed it to the floor. They even pulled out everything inside the chest one by one, broke them to pieces and went away!

They left without finding the entrance to the underground city.

But how?

The hatch should have been laid bare and defenseless in Niaz hideout's closet right before their eyes! How did not they see it?

Faraz . . .

When Asij and Hedayat passed through the city entrance and went down the stairs, Faraz went to Niaz's den from the coffee shop's roof. Then he jumped down and entered the den. He headed straight to the closet. He realized that the hatch was shut but pieces of cement were scattered all over the place. He did not have enough time. He acted quickly, opened the hatch and using Niaz's broken and worn out broom, poured any traces that could give away the hatch into it. Then he shut the hatch close. He pulled the rug over the hatch and put the chest on the rug. He had finished his job and crossed his fingers.

- "Let's luck do the rest."

He hastily climbed the hideout's wall and with great difficulty and hid in the dark.

Luck helped too.

****

The Ancient Passageway

The exit pathway was in the middle of the rocky mountain in the midst of a large gap. The outlet was covered with plenty of bushes and weeds. The vegetation coverage was so massive that it made a lot of trouble for both Asij and Hedayat as they got out. Asij, while holding a large black bag and grabbing Hedayat with the other hand, groaned impatiently and tiredly, "The guys went over the top to hide this place! We had no hope of continuing our way if they had tried a bit harder!"

"How long should we walk, sir?" asked Hedayat.

They had walked underground for a day and night. Sometimes the road was bumpy and sometimes a sticky mud coating covered the passageway and one's hand sank into the mud when one touched the walls. According to Asij, that road had the advantage that no one was in it! The lad was tired, his face was pale and he looked tired. But every time Asij took a step forward, it was more robust and

joyful than the previous step. Even now that the legs felt
feeble, the mouth was dry and the eyes were dim, a big
smile shone on his face.

He almost shouted cheerfully and happily, "A little! We are
very close, prince!" and as he grabbed the lad's hand to pull
him up through a crack in the rock, added, "If the surface
is filled with dirt and sludge, we have to travel
underground."

He pulled up Hedayat and shook clean the lad's brown
jacket from dirt and mud and weed, "We are almost there,
dear. Look, we are far from everything."

They stood on the edge of a gap in the middle of the
mountain. They could see the backside of Obliso. The
backside of Obliso was shinier. More lively and without
any grooves or tracks.

Obliso was the furthest place the boy could imagine. But
this third mountain . . . never. On the right side of the two
travelers, a stone passageway could be seen from the
middle of the mountain. It was as if someone with a steel
chisel and chip-ax had carved every foot of it. The
passageway gently turned around the mountain and went
down and disappeared somewhere between the third
mountain and the brown hills.

On the other side of the brown hills, a few patches of white
cotton clouds shone in the sky. Down below, there was the
plain. Sometimes a hill, sometimes a marshland . . . and in
distant, a cityscape's gray mirage.

****

Welcome

Behind them, there were the old woman and the old man, Parishan and many memorabilia of the inn and coffee shop, which could persuade Hedayat to return. Ahead, there was an unknown world that Asij had talked so much about it. They went down the stone steps. Each step was an indication of getting away, of not seeing anymore, of new hardships. Will it be worth it? Those new hardships that he did not know anything about? Ask Asij to know what would be his answer?

- "Yes, yes, yes. It is so unspeakably valuable. I do not want to exaggerate but there is fate. It is our last hope. It is the future, *the* future. Like many people who do not care about anything, we could bask beside the fire flame in the winter and on the porch of a building in a good climate in the summer; and laugh without concern and the fear of the future. Pile up money and call it happiness. But we are not like that. Awareness means knocking on a gate that opens into hell."

They reached the brown hills when the sun - red and worn out - was ready to set. Our men walked ahead under the horizon's red glow. Asij was leading the way. They descended the hill in the dark and between the third mountain and the brown hill, came to a road covered with pebbles. Asij stopped and got some rest. It seemed that he had just remembered something called fatigue.

He asked Hedayat, "Sometimes I think I am getting old, is it not it? Please say no!"

He stepped back a few steps to stand next to Hedayat, bending down to be equal to Hedayat: "Look . . . what you see? Well, you see nothing because it is dark all over. Your life in the coffee shop was like this."

He turned the flashlight on and pointed its light ahead. The road lit up and a large gap appeared in the mountain on their right. Asij continued, "But the fact that you wanted to be here and left the inn and coffee shop, is like turning on the flashlight here. When you have eyes, you do not search in the darkness. You wanted light, light."

Hedayat remembered Parishan and asked, "Did Parishan stay there?"

Asij lowered his head and replied blankly, "My brother was part of the story. A lot of good things would not have been possible without him. Even you might not have been here and probably I. Parishan sees the light . . . however, his method did not work very well. Sitting and chanting only works to calm down your own heart. It is easy for the disabled elderly. The outside world goes its own way."

They walked toward the large gap. Little by little, they went far from the brown hills and sank deep into the heart of the mountain. After a few minutes of walking, they reached a rocky cavity. A large and circular place, wide and spacious. There was a big tent in the middle of the square. On the two sides of its door, which welcomed our men, two great fires were burning. There was a sign similar to an insignia on Asij's coat on both sides of the flaming torches. Asij shouted out loud with confidence, "Peace be upon you . . ."

****

The Last Bastion of Resistance

A black and stylish fabric structure was set up like a circus tent in a large square in the heart of the third mountain. Its wide entrance was nicely decorated and the tent was shaped like a glorious helmet. Two long silver horns had twisted and rose above the huge tent on both sides. A vague face and a frown were on its forehead. Two eyes whose pupils seemed to have been eroded over time, and finally, a broad snout and wide mouth that connected to the tent entrance.

Our heroes, one tiny and skinny, and the other tall and huge, entered along with a bunch of men and women wearing vibrant and colorful clothing.

The inside was bright and crowded. The men and women who entered in their company scattered. From the heart of the brightness, a short and bald man with a neat and kind face emerged. He limped a little and looked sick.

- "Peace be upon you, great and powerful Asij . . . and peace be upon you . . . our dear guest. Welcome, my dear."

Four women appeared from behind that man. They wore long silk clothes. Their long brown hair covered their chests on both sides of their shawls, like willow tree branches.

Asij removed his hat and said, "Peace be upon you, dear Mehrban. We are tired, hungry, thirsty and exhausted," he pointed to Hedayat and added, "Protect Hedayat, protect our treasure, Mehrban" and went away and disappeared in the crowd's gladness and greetings.

It was full of amazing animals, ranging from monkeys to peacocks and white horses and playful rabbits. Tools that Hedayat had never seen in his life. Not just Hedayat, but nobody except the people in the fortress knew what they are. Every part of it had a different color and design. Hedayat was looking around flabbergasted and got the exciting time and again by seeing those things.

- "Have not you seen anything like this before, my dear?" asked the short man with a big and sympathetic smile.

Hedayat shook his head no.

The man grabbed Hedayat's hand and took him into the crowd as he limped.

- "Welcome to the magical animals' sector, dear!"

The man stroked a monkey's head, took something out of his pocket and gave it to the animal. He pulled Hedayat behind him and introduced Hedayat to every animal that came by.

- "Hey, Aban Bano . . . this little gentleman is our new guest! Look how kind and good he is."

And stroked the white horse's mane. He made Hedayat familiar with each new section as they walked.

- "My dear Mr. Hedayat, we are a team. A good and skilled team. Look at that girl," he pointed to one of the three ladies that Hedayat had seen before, "She is the best knife thrower in the world. Blindfolded, can you believe it? She hits the mark blindfolded."

They nudged open their way among men and women and advanced. He took Hedayat to his room, which unlike other places, was free of people and animals.

Hedayat's head was spinning by seeing all those strange things.

He seated Hedayat on the edge of the bed and stood there facing him, "Traveling with me – perhaps – could be a bit boring and troublesome. I am afflicted with arthritis disease, gentleman. To the extent that sometimes it is difficult for me to walk. The occasional headaches have driven me and the people around me up to the wall. But . . . with all these misfortunes, I am a frequent traveler. We are going to find something together. It could be on the other side of the world! We look for bits and pieces of truth in this show . . . you have a role, and I have a role too. Do you know what is my role in this show?"

Hedayat thought for a moment, scratched his face, and said, "A friend of horses and monkeys?"

"No, no, no, oh, god. I am the clown here. Is it not funny?!" He picked up a green box from the tarpaulin niche and opened it. He dipped his finger in it and rubbed it to Hedayat's nose. Hedayat's nose turned red. He smeared Hedayat's lips on both sides. He wiped his finger with his shirt. He took the black color from the color box and rubbed it to Hedayat's eyebrows. He took out a mirror from his pocket (a round mirror with many paints on its backside) and held it in front of Hedayat. What Hedayat saw in the mirror made him feel a special sensation? Not joy, not grief, not anger and not kindness.

****

Bringing the missing pieces together

The sun emerged in the midst of the dark, cloudy gray space. The sun rays illuminated the third mountain entirely. They call that the beginning of the day.

The day, from the window of the clown's room, slowly splashed on his brown tarpaulin wall. This day was different from all other days of the clown. It had begun with a promise for him. He had to narrate. He was very skilled in fiction writing and storytelling. He wrote the plays; all fiction narratives were his work. He was not just a clown, but a writer clown.

In the vague and endless nights, he took the pen and wrote. When the whole team, fell asleep under a warm blanket, put their heads on a soft pillow and drowned in a dream or nightmare; he created characters with the help of his words, put together the missing pieces and made a narrative, wrote a story, and . . . . Now he had vowed to narrate.

****

Towards the next station

In less than an hour, the tent was disassembled. The tools and equipment were loaded on the large and old truck and there was nothing left of the lodging of fifty diverse people, except a few holes and cracks and small wounds all over the ground.

Mehrban shouted orders. Everyone had something in hand and ran around. The team members got on blue, green and yellow vans in a short while. Eventually, the vans began to move. They drove slowly on the gravel and then went down the sandy road.

Asij, Mehrban, and Hedayat, the last people left behind the caravan, walked alongside each other. Asij carefully examined the surroundings, filled the holes and removed the remaining traces, "No one should know anything about us being here!"

He smiled at Hedayat.

Mehrban said while almost dragging his feet on the ground, "Oh, yes, yes, dear Asij, you are right, oh!"

Asij put his hand on Hedayat's shoulder and gave him something. Then he said, "We are going to the town. We will set up the tent near the town and people will come to see us."

Mehrban went to the black Jeep. Asij carefully checked the area to find the last holes and traces and quickened his pace.

Hedayat has left along among them.

Asij shouted from the distance, "Let's go."

The lad stood in a stunning square in the focal point of a deep cleft at the heart of the third mountain. He looked at the white clouds overhead. He had a book in hand and thought of something that to be aware of it one must . . .

The End

www.ingramcontent.com/pod-product-compliance
Lightning Source LLC
Chambersburg PA
CBHW060358050426
42449CB00009B/1798